"Rod's playbook is a must rec
anyone aspiring to be

Mary Poppen, CCO at involve.ai and former CC

THE CHIEF CUSTOMER OFFICER PLAYBOOK

8 STRATEGIES THAT WILL ACCELERATE YOUR CAREER AND WIN YOU A SEAT AT THE EXECUTIVE TABLE

ROD CHERKAS

Foreword by Nick Mehta - *CEO, Gainsight*

Preface by Gemma Cipriani-Espineira - *CCO, Chili Piper*

Publishing Process by Weston Lyon
www.PlugAndPlayPublishing.com

Book Cover by Dave Praetorius | www.LisaLarter.com

Graphics by Sharon Holmes and
Tracey Miller | design@traceofstyle.com

Developmental Editing by Dan Janal
Line Editing by Jenny Butterfield Lyon

ISBN: 9798370212383

To my beautiful wife, Corey, for being my favorite person, my adventure buddy, and for encouraging me to pursue my dreams.

To my parents, who were always my biggest fans. They showed me what it meant to be a kind person and to deliver great experiences, one smile (dentist) and garment (dry cleaner) at a time.

To you – the reader – the CCOs, the aspiring CCOs along with the investors, CEOs, and peer executives. Thank you for inspiring me to create this resource for you.

What Others Are Saying About *The CCO Playbook*

"Rod's playbook is a must read for CCOs and anyone aspiring to be a CCO."

-Mary Poppen, CCO at involve.ai and
former CCO at SAP and LinkedIn

"By far the best book of the year."

-Chris Hicken, CEO at 'nuffsaid

"Rod's playbook is going to be the future North Star for how CCOs operate."

-Kellie Capote, Chief Customer Officer at Gainsight

"Rod has written the playbook to help guide the future generation of Chief Customer Officers on what the role looks like and the path to get there. He offers a perspective that I don't think anybody else has in the industry."

-Kate Peter, Head of Customer Success
at Harvard Business Publishing

"Rod's book is a must read for those looking to understand the role of the CCO and what skills and experience you need to accumulate in your career to attain a CCO position."

-Michael Horsley, Director of Customer Success at Hyperscience

"Cherkas has written a powerful playbook not only for CCOs but the entire executive team. It's a new game, and the CCO is the customers' advocate."

-Michael Gospe, Customer Advisory Board Strategist and Interim CMO, KickStart Alliance

"An amazing resource for CCOs, aspiring post-sale leaders, as well as CEOs hiring or managing CCOs."

-Srikrishnan Ganesan, Co-Founder at Rocketlane

"Rod's book provides a model and structure for how the CCO role can radically enhance the financial performance of his or her company while staying squarely focused on delivering value and delighting customers."

-Robert Padron, Chief Growth Officer at Arise Virtual Solutions

"Rod's playbook does a fantastic job. It decodes all the CCO responsibilities and provides tangible suggestions to navigate your career to become a world class CCO."

-Angie Holt, Chief Customer Officer at Productiv

"This is the book that has been missing not only for aspiring CCOs but to educate the business world about the importance of a CCO. I have not seen a career framework for senior leaders like this before."

-Jennifer Baca, Manager of Enterprise Customer Success at Zoom

"Now there is a tangible playbook that can help you get to the C-Suite."

-Nicole Alrubaiy, VP of Customer Success at Clari

"This book will help you make your CEO and your CFO look good. It will make your CEO say, 'This person is going someplace and maybe they can be my replacement.' "

-Omid Razavi, Chief Advocacy Officer at SupportLogic

"This is a fantastic resource that I would classify as required reading for any aspiring leader in the Customer Success or Post-Sale world. I love the specific, actionable recommendations and the many real-life examples from CCOs and CS leaders."

-Laurence Leong, VP of Customer Success at Jamf

"Rod's book is the ideal guide for anyone considering a C-level, customer-facing role as his or her next career move. It is an indispensable, practical guide to successfully grow into the role of CCO."

-Hannah Thompson, Chief Operating Officer at Finastra

"As a recently promoted CCO, this book really helped me to understand more about my role and how I can provide the most valuable impact to my company. I am sure that Rod's book will help other leaders in the same way. It is a must-read for every Customer Success leader, no matter what role they have."

-Marko Müller, Chief Customer Officer at Staffbase

"We don't have a school for how to do Customer Success and Services. There really are few mentors out there. Rod brings that guidance, expertise, and value."

-Inger Rarick, SVP of Customer Success at Sendoso

"I loved this book! It provides a framework for the key attributes of a great CCO and a tactical path on how to get to this level. I felt myself nodding my head as I read through each page."

-Star Hofer, Chief Customer Officer, PartnerStack

"On every page, I felt there was something of special interest to me or useful content. Rod has written a great book!"

-Paula Sobb, SVP of Customer Success at Sinch

"*The CCO Playbook* demystifies core concepts and tasks required to grow into the CCO role."

-Karla Kannan, Senior Vice President of Customer Experience at BirchStreet

"The writing is clear, concise, and action oriented. Rod has a great book."

-Christine Rimer, Chief Customer Officer at Guideline

"I enjoyed the pace and the progressive layout of so many relevant customer experience topics. Rod's voice shines through, making this book interesting and not academic."

-Mathilde Sanson, Chief Customer Officer at Black Swan Data

"I would recommend that anyone going up for a promotion read this book."

-Laura Lakhwara, Director of Customer Success at UIPath

"Rod's book was an engaging read. The strategic framework is easy to follow with all the little tips and tricks. It allowed me to reflect on my career path. I found myself creating my own action plan as I read each chapter."

-Tiffany Taylor, Director of EDU Success and Education at Handshake

"This book fills a huge gap with detailed, actionable and proven insights into the emerging CCO role. There is no one better than Rod to have taken on this challenge."

-Amit Kandpal, Customer Success Leader at Netskope

"Rod takes decades of knowledge and condenses it into a consumable book so we all can benefit."

-Mike Lee, Director of Customer Success at PublicInput

"Rod has written an effective guide that demystifies the potential paths to CCO. It provides actionable insights, thought leadership, and a strategic roadmap to get there."

-Ben Collier, VP of Expert Services at Amplience

"This book gives you tangible exercises. I also like the real-world examples."

-Brian Hartley, Senior Director of Customer Success at RFP360

Table of Contents

Foreword

I have known Rod Cherkas for almost ten years. Our professional and personal friendship started during his time at Marketo, where his company was one of Gainsight's first dozen customers. I got to know Rod even more closely when he worked at Gainsight, leading our Professional Services and Education organizations. I was always impressed by his tireless advocacy for the Customer Success community, his ability to design and execute innovative customer experiences, and his willingness to share his knowledge with other customer-facing executives.

Of all the things I have discussed with Rod over the years, the one I am most excited about is his desire to add structure, best practices, and career development frameworks to the role of a Chief Customer Officer.

As the CEO of Gainsight, I have witnessed trends such as the exponential growth of the Customer Success community and the evolving expectations for this relatively new CCO role. My team and I at Gainsight have written several books that established a set of frameworks and principles for what it takes to operate a Customer Success organization and to develop a career as a Customer Success professional.

Employees at your company are watching the signals you send in the structure of your executive team. You care about people, so you have a Chief People Officer. You have a Chief Financial Officer because your financial results are important. Your customers also need "a seat at the table," through a Chief Customer Officer. I believe that every company across almost every industry should have an executive that is a peer to your Sales, Marketing, Finance, Product, and other leaders.

Until now, there has not been a book that focused on what aspiring Chief Customers Officers can do to accelerate their career path or what existing Chief Customer Officers can do to maximize their impact for their customers, team members, and their company. Rod's ideas are easy to understand and put into practice. He shares compelling stories from successful CCOs, board members, and evolving customer-facing leaders. He offers actionable tips to help you be more effective in your daily work and to help you demonstrate your value to your customers and your organization.

The ideas in *The Chief Customer Officer Playbook* are not just for technology start-ups and scale-ups. They are relevant for any customer-facing leader or executive across all types of industries and company sizes. CEOs and Board Members should also read this book to know what to expect from their Chief Customer Officers. Other C-Suite executives should read it to know how best to collaborate with their peers.

There is no better person I can think of than Rod to write this book. The strategic roadmap he shares for CCOs and aspiring CCOs has never been more relevant. I am glad that Rod is sharing his insight and experience with us.

I'm fired up to hear your reaction!

Nick Mehta
CEO, Gainsight
Palo Alto, California
January 2023

Preface

This playbook provides the fast track I wish I had when I became a Chief Customer Officer. Most of the literature out there today on what it takes to become a CCO is very customer-experience-focused. Rod fills this gap by having a playbook that talks directly to anyone that wants to become a CCO or to CCOs who want to improve their business results.

When you're trying to become a CCO, it's helpful to talk to people who have been there. The problem is finding them. Customer-facing executives are still the exception rather than the norm. Traditionally, CCOs have risen via the Customer Experience (CX) world or start by gaining all their experience at larger companies which they can transfer to smaller startups willing to provide them with a C-level title. As a VP of Customer Success forging my path to the C-Suite via fast-growing businesses, I didn't have peers on the same path to learn from. And learning at the pace of my own experience was not fast enough.

So, I took a highly academic, research-driven approach to learning how the best do what they do. I launched *Chief Customer Officer Secrets*, a YouTube series where I spoke to

Customer Executives about their roles and how they got to where they are today. This is how I met Rod. One of the leaders I serve on my team worked with Rod and had amazing things to say about him.

Rod and I immediately bonded over our shared passion to help customer-facing leaders get a seat at the executive table. Rod gives actionable advice clearly and compassionately, drawing from his research and experiences across companies of different sizes. Rod knows the difficulties of the role. He helped me articulate how a CCO is critical to the strategic vision of a company. Rod encouraged me to balance short and long-term thinking, so I could shatter new standards of service without letting the day-to-day take me away from it all. This mindset has been critical to ensuring I can meet the immediate needs of my customers while shaping the vision of the business.

This book is the all-in-one-place blueprint for you to go and start experimenting with best practices. I'm excited about what this means for an industry of people who dedicate their careers to helping others. And I'm grateful to Rod for setting a stunning example of what it looks like to "let the ladder" down so others can shine.

Gemma Cipriani-Espineira
Chief Customer Officer, Chili Piper
Connecticut, USA
January 2023

Read This First

In September 2021, Yamini Rangan, the Chief Customer Officer of the sales and marketing software company Hubspot, was announced as its new Chief Executive Officer. Those of us who work in post-sale functions celebrated the ascension of one of our own to the top role at such a fast-growing, publicly-traded company. Rangan had been a very successful executive during her time at Hubspot after moving from Dropbox where she was also the Chief Customer Officer. It shouldn't have been such a big deal. But there just haven't been very many, if any, prominent Chief Customer Officers that have been promoted to CEO.

It got me wondering "why?" Reflecting back on one of the major benefits of Hubspot's original value proposition, it looked like a "pipeline problem." Just like high-value clients don't just materialize at your company, Chief Customer Officers also need to be nurtured and grown through their career journeys. This still-evolving leadership role can deliver tremendous value to customer outcomes and company valuation, but the skills and competencies need to be acquired and honed over time.

After further research, I discovered that until now, no one has documented how aspiring customer-facing leaders can predictably assemble the skills and experiences over the course of their careers so they can confidently become Chief Customer Officers. I also uncovered that once leaders ascend to executive-level roles in these customer-facing functions, they find a very limited set of best practices, frameworks, and stories to help guide their strategic decision-making and operational execution. This book will give you that roadmap and the set of resources you will need.

The Chief Customer Officer position is still a pretty new executive title with relatively few high-visibility role models. Plus there is limited documentation as to "what works." So people in these leadership positions often end up "winging it," putting themselves at risk of missing opportunities to learn from the proven practices and the experience of others. That has been my own experience many times. I can assure you that "winging it" doesn't always work out so well, and that approach leaves you with battle scars.

The Chief Customer Officer Playbook addresses those gaps. It offers Chief Customer Officers and those who aspire to be Chief Customer Officers a roadmap for how to scale their businesses and their careers so they can earn and keep a seat at the executive table. This book helps you, as a post-sale leader at any level in your organization, feel more confident you can achieve better outcomes in your current role while pointing out opportunities to accelerate your career growth.

Wherever you are in the customer-facing leadership journey, I have been in your shoes. I have managed front-line teams in functions including technical support, professional services, success management, and more for Intuit, Marketo, Gainsight, and RingCentral, among others. I have also been responsible for the entire customer-facing journey reporting to the CEO several times. Now I lead the consulting firm, HelloCCO, which partners with Chief Customer Officers and their leadership teams to design, execute and scale their post-sale organizations across a variety of industries. My work with my clients helps them increase retention rates, implement new clients faster, scale efficiently, leverage partners, and expand existing client relationships to accelerate revenue growth. This all leads to increased shareholder value.

I am lucky to have worked at companies that placed tremendous value on designing and delivering great customer experiences. However, I can confidently say that leading an organization that is "customer-focused" or "customer-obsessed" or "customer-whatevered" is not enough. You also need to deliver operational results that are measurable, impactful, and scalable. If you want to be the type of leader that can be successful at a high-performing company, you should keep reading.

The Chief Customer Officer Playbook is written so you can easily follow the tips and best practices that you will need to grow in your career. Whether you are currently a Chief Customer Officer, aspire to be a Chief Customer Officer, or are a manager in one of the post-sale functions in a growing organization, you will find impactful and relevant stories, case studies, and best practices that are unique to customer-facing leaders like yourself.

Along the way, you will also pick up management principles that will enable you to be a more effective leader as you scale your team and contribute to company growth. This book provides a roadmap for you to build a set of competencies, skills, and experiences that are enjoyable, impactful, and meaningful. You can also use the topics and chapters of this book as discussion starters with your teams to improve performance.

How This Book Is Structured

This book has three parts:

Part 1: The Evolution and Role of the Chief Customer Officer – We will explore the evolving role of the Chief Customer Officer and the expanding impact this leadership position has on your company's operating results. We will discover what functions are most commonly under the responsibility of a Chief Customer Officer and how these teams work together to deliver value for employees, customers, and shareholders. We will also highlight the critical success metrics and key performance indicators for each part of the organization.

Part 2: The Path to Becoming a Chief Customer Officer – We will highlight the skills and competencies that are important for CCOs and aspiring CCOs to develop. We will leverage a framework for a CCO Maturity Model™ that helps you as an evolving leader evaluate where you are on eight important dimensions. The framework also gives you a tool to track your progress along your career and build a roadmap for continuing to develop the appropriate competencies in the future.

We will highlight real-life examples of how leaders like you tackle the opportunities you will face in your business. You will learn actionable tips and best practices to help you anticipate your future challenges, see around corners, and put in place the strategic improvements you will need so you can be ready to meet your evolving business needs.

Part 3: Action Plan and Trends to Consider – You can take the opportunity to define your own action plan that outlines specific steps to accelerate progress along your career path. You can create a timeline with action items and create your own personal CCO Playbook. We also discuss a number of trends and predictions that you should keep an eye on over the coming years.

Tips for Reading This Book

Throughout this book, you will notice that key insights, tips, and best practices are highlighted to make it easier for you to recall and apply these principles. These are based on the experiences of dozens of Chief Customer Officers and hundreds of post-sale leaders, managers, and front-line team members as well as my own experiences. While your day-to-day routines may be challenging, learning how to do your job better should be easy. You'll recognize these callouts quickly by these icons:

Career Accelerators – Career accelerators are examples of decisions, development opportunities, and experiences that often have a way of propelling you forward in your career. They may introduce you to new skills, expose you to important decisions, or offer opportunities for interacting with key peers, executives, or customers that can positively influence your growth. Remember the game *Chutes and Ladders* you may have played when you were a kid? These are the Ladders.

Pitfalls – Every job has its challenging situations. Leading a post-sale organization or being a Chief Customer Officer is no different. Throughout this book, you will be exposed to examples of particularly challenging decisions that you may face in your organization. The good news is that after reading this book, you will be better equipped to anticipate the pitfalls far enough ahead of time to find ways to avoid them. These challenging situations are the Chutes.

Metrics That Matter – One of the primary trends over the past few years for Chief Customer Officers and their post-sale teams is the expectation for their organizations to deliver consistent, measurable results that tie back to company goals. In this book, you will learn examples of how you and your organization can measure outcomes so that you can demonstrate the value you provide to your customers and the impact your organization has on company performance.

Trends to Watch – Throughout this book, I point out certain areas where change is occurring or where new ideas are developing. You will want to pay particular attention to these changes to determine how they could impact your business.

At the end of each chapter, I provide you with a short set of questions for you to consider as you develop your own action plan for each topic. You can use them as prompts for yourself or you can use them as discussion starters with your team or manager. I share recommendations for specific steps you can take to develop the particular skills and accelerate your career growth.

You will also get access to a set of worksheets, resources, and frameworks that you can use. Feel free to write directly in this book. You don't have time for double data-entry, right?

Mostly, I hope that you find this book to be a very practical resource to help you navigate the opportunities you have to contribute to the growth of your organization while also developing your career. The role of a Chief Customer Officer has become one that requires an exciting combination of strong operational execution with effective strategic planning skills. *The Chief Customer Officer Playbook* can be your companion on your career journey to get yourself on track to becoming an outstanding Chief Customer Officer. Let me know how it goes.

Rod Cherkas
January 2023
San Mateo, CA
rod@hellocco.com
www.rodcherkas.com

Part 1

The Evolution and Role of the Chief Customer Officer

The Evolution of the Chief Customer Officer

There has never been a better time to be a Chief Customer Officer. If you like to help customers win and your company grow, the CCO role is a dream job. Chief Customer Officers are held in high regard by their company's executive team, command high salaries that reflect their growing value, and have recently earned a seat at the executive table. Post-Sale executives who can contribute directly to top-line revenue growth and bottom-line profitability improvements add tremendous value to their companies and garner enviable recognition from their CEOs and CFOs.

Chief Customer Officers play an increasingly important executive role because they are accountable for achieving important financial results while also connecting the dots across a range of mission-critical, customer-facing functions. They act as the cross-functional champion for internal initiatives that improve customer experiences and outcomes. They advocate for the needs of your customers to your peer leaders and organizations. Plus, they are constantly looking for new ways to make things even better for your customers in the future.

If achieving these outcomes is important to your company, you could probably benefit from having a Chief Customer Officer.

The challenge is that there just aren't that many of us around yet. According to LinkedIn, there are currently only a few more than 4,000 people with Chief Customer Officer titles in the world. That compares to over 57,000 Chief Marketing Officers and over 200,000 Chief Financial Officers. The number of CFOs alone tells you that most companies are focused clearly on their bottom line. Together, we need to expand the pipeline of aspiring CCOs and add an all-important customer lens to the operations of companies around the world and across a wide range of industries.

The role of the Chief Customer Officer has evolved significantly over the past decade in a way that dramatically expanded the scope and impact of the position. No longer is the CCO responsible solely for the strategy, design, and execution of the customer experiences that make up what is often referred to as the "customer journey." That responsibility is certainly still a primary component of the job.

But now, the CCO is also expected to operate as an executive-level business owner who is accountable for driving financial results that significantly impact shareholder value. The Chief

Customer Officer role has also expanded to new industries including technology, financial services, hospitality, business services, and health care. Post-sale leaders that can successfully combine their passion for improving customer outcomes with the management prowess to achieve this in a financially efficient and scalable way can become superstars.

TRENDS TO WATCH

CCOs are increasingly responsible for delivering financial results and managing large organizations.

The Early Days of the CCO Role

In the years between 2010 and 2015, investors generally rewarded companies for delivering strong top-line revenue growth. As long as revenue growth was high, investors were less concerned about the amount of spending required to acquire, activate, and retain their customers. Company valuations were commonly measured as a multiple of their revenue and their revenue growth rate. There was an inherent faith that profitability could be achieved at some point in the future. Or maybe investors at the time just didn't care as much about profitability.

The Chief Customer Officer type of role at that time was commonly responsible for helping to design the customer experiences that could fuel this revenue growth. At some companies, leaders held titles like Chief Customer Experience

Officer or VP of Customer Care. One of their primary responsibilities was gathering "Voice of the Customer" input from various "listening posts" across the organization and trying to make sense of it for the many internal functional teams like product, marketing, and sales. In many cases, leaders in these roles had relatively small teams and often had limited ability to directly influence the operational execution of their strategies and recommendations.

One of the primary measures of success during those early years of the decade was the Net Promoter Score™ (NPS). This metric became not only a target Key Performance Indicator (KPI) for this customer-facing executive leader but often became a target for the entire company's executive team. However, assigning accountability for improving a metric like NPS was difficult. There were so many different inputs that could drive the NPS score up or down over time – product functionality, sales expectations, implementation experience, support response times, ease of use, and more. There was constant finger-pointing among functional leaders and no accountability. The Chief Customer Officer, Chief Experience Officer, or Customer Care leader were organizational influencers but not major contributors to the growth of shareholder value.

The Rise of Retention as a Key Performance Indicator After 2015

By 2015, an entirely new role had gained traction, starting in recurring revenue software companies and later expanding into a wider range of industries. This was the role of a Customer Success Manager and a Success Management team. Customer Success software company Gainsight, led by their charismatic CEO, Nick Mehta, had developed a software solution that helped organizations track and manage all of their customer-facing interactions in a single place. More importantly, Gainsight's software enabled Post-Sale leaders for the first time to directly tie the work of their teams to a new metric that their company wanted to optimize – customer retention.

At the same time, investors began to move away from valuing companies based primarily on revenue growth. Increasingly, they were now expecting companies to grow *efficiently*. This meant focusing more on the unit economics of not only acquiring a customer but also retaining and growing its existing ones. It became widely recognized that retaining a customer was much less expensive than letting those current customers churn and then spending money to replace the lost customers. This goal to increase retention was what became known as "fixing the leaky bucket."

Nick Mehta and his team at Gainsight capitalized on this trend and championed the creation of a new organizational function to optimize customer retention rates. They advocated for the role of a Customer Success Manager (CSM) that worked directly with clients to ensure that customers were receiving the value they expected from their purchases. They also championed for Customer Success to become a new company discipline.

"Customer Success is a philosophy, and it must pervade the entire company," Mehta wrote in his landmark 2016 book, *Customer Success*. "No organization, or job role, can function in a vacuum, and customer success may be the best example of this. It requires a top-down commitment to truly deliver world-class customer success."

I was working at Marketo during Gainsight's very early days. Marketo became one of Gainsight's first ten customers. So I had a front-row seat to the early growth of this entire software category and the ascendency of the Customer Success related professions. Many years later, I joined Gainsight as their Vice President of Global Professional Services.

The premise behind Gainsight's worldview was that by closely managing the customer's experience and ability to recognize value, a business could increase the likelihood of retaining that customer and growing its relationship with them. In addition, this mindset of driving retention and expansion could be relevant across many industries – from software to financial services to business services to hospitality. By 2020, the role of Customer Success Manager (CSM) was recognized as the fastest growing job title by LinkedIn. There were over 80,000 new CSM roles created between 2015 and 2020.

The leader of this new organization of Customer Success Managers was frequently called the Customer Success leader. Depending on scope, this person might be a senior manager, director level, or VP level title. This individual managed teams that were responsible for collaborating with customers and delivering experiences that helped improve retention rates and product adoption.

Over time, these Customer Success organizations started to recognize that through their direct interactions with their customers, they were not just able to influence whether clients chose to stay as a customer. When customer relationships were well developed, Customer Success teams were also able to identify opportunities for how their customers could expand their use of the product or solution across their company. They could apply their company's product or service to more use cases. They could sell more licenses. They could consume the solution more frequently. The leader's role of this Success Management organization was expanding. They were expected to contribute to the retention and now the revenue expansion of existing customers.

Along came a new metric called Net Revenue Retention (NRR) that calculates the percentage of revenue retained from customers over a period of time including account expansions and downsells. Investors loved this metric as it tied directly back to their desire to see companies grow efficiently. It provided a way to measure how much growth companies could expect to see from their existing base of customers. Not only that but it could also be benchmarked against competitors within your segment as well as across industries.

Net Retention Rate has quickly become one of the top three metrics tracked for inclusion at board meetings, investor calls, and SEC filings right behind Sales Growth and Profit Margin. Companies can also calculate the lifetime value (LTV) of a customer more easily.

METRICS THAT MATTER

Net Revenue Retention has become a key metric for many companies and investors.

Identifying Inputs to Customer Retention and Growth

Post-Sale executives quickly realized that there were a wide variety of input factors that contributed to the Net Revenue Retention Rate. Not all these factors were directly managed solely by this newly evolving Success Management function.

Customer onboarding was identified as one of the most important factors that correlated to high retention rates. Customers who use the company's solution early and often begin to recognize its value quickly, increasing the likelihood of renewals and upgrades. In some technology companies, these onboarding services were delivered by team members that worked in groups that might have names like the Onboarding team, the Enablement team, the Implementation team, or the Professional Services team. Sometimes onboarding services are provided by third-party partners or contractors, adding yet another dimension to getting customers started using the company's solutions quickly and successfully. In other situations, the products did not require any implementation support at all. Customers were able to use the solutions without any assistance or they could use the documentation and training resources made available by the vendor.

New users often had to learn how to use the company's products or services. Working with a Professional Services resource or a Customer Success Manager (CSM) to get trained could be costly and inefficient, particularly for some segments of customers. So, self-service training resources and education courses were often required to provide simple learning paths to enable customers and help them expand their adoption.

Another common factor for customer churn was the quality of the service or experience. Support organizations were the front line in addressing these types of issues. For many companies, this included a combination of self-service frequently asked questions, knowledge base articles, customer communities, and access to higher-touch support resources in chat, phone, and email. For larger clients, some companies even established higher value support service offerings that could provide a premium level of attention for their most valuable clients. Support organizations were no longer just cost centers, but they could now be seen as contributors to growth through this Net Revenue Retention metric.

CHAPTER REVIEW

This new evolution of a Chief Customer Officer would need to be strategic yet operationally strong. These new CCOs would need to be empathetic with customers yet financially fluent. They would need to be able to translate investments in improving experiences into measurable financial results. They would have an opportunity to be an equal partner to other executive-level leaders to drive company growth.

Congratulations! You are in for an exciting time as this role expands, grows, and becomes even more important for your company. I cannot wait for you to tell me stories of how your career has progressed. Enjoy the journey.

In the next chapter, we will define the scope of responsibility for a Chief Customer Officer. This book will help you earn and keep your seat at the executive table by enabling you to identify, develop, and master the eight skills you need to be a successful Chief Customer Officer.

The Scope of the CCO Role

So, what is expected from a Chief Customer Officer? In researching this book, many past and current CCOs provided their perspectives and advice. There were several common themes regarding the skills and behaviors that CCOs are expected to demonstrate – take the big picture company perspective, understand how all the different functions at a company contribute to financial results, integrate feedback from various parts of the customer journey, and bring the client's perspective out to the company.

Eduarda Camacho is the very successful Chief Customer Officer of BMC, a publicly held global enterprise software and services company with over 9,000 employees. She believes that the most important role of a CCO is to bring a customer perspective to the many different functions of the company. Her advice for aspiring leaders is that if you want to be a CCO, you cannot just be a leader for your own customer-facing teams. You need to bring more to the table. A CCO needs to understand the whole company and how the disparate functions work together to deliver value.

"You have to know your functional space, but you also have to understand product and HR and Finance and Sales. One of the things that benefited me was that I worked in so many different organizations. I was able to connect the dots pretty well," she said.

"I started to really make sure that I understood what was happening behind each of those functions because then I could present the customer to each function. You can speak each department's language for why something they need to do differently is right for the customer."

Other influential Chief Customer Officers also recognized the value that this evolving CCO role could have to drive company-level outcomes.

Dan Steinman was the first Chief Customer Officer at Gainsight, the software company that is credited with championing the Customer Success movement. He is also the co-author with Nick Mehta of *Customer Success: How Innovative Companies Are Reducing Churn and Growing Recurring Revenue.*

Dan has had a front-row seat to the evolution of the customer success movement and the changing expectations of a Chief Customer Officer. He believes that the role of the CCO is a complex, mission-critical position that is accountable for overseeing and optimizing across a number of different departments.

He says that "CCOs often manage Support, Professional Services, Onboarding, Customer Success, and maybe renewals and training. I contend that the CCO job is a challenging role. Every one of these organizations is measured differently. It is much better training for becoming a CEO."

Steinman's advice to aspiring CCOs is to be willing (and possibly even eager) to take roles in different functional organizations throughout their careers. This helps you learn how each of these functions operates. "When you are a CCO, your CEO is really saying to you, 'Here are a whole bunch of people, so figure out how to deliver the outcome we want at the lowest possible cost. I don't care how you organize it. It is about utilizing your resources in the best possible way.'"

"An experienced CEO knows that the customer part of the equation is not only as important as new product sales but in the long run is way more important to the business," Steinman says. "If new business sales miss the goal number by 10%, it hardly affects the bottom line. The only thing that matters is net retention and gross retention, which is heavily weighted on the side of customers."

Responsibilities and Expectations For a Chief Customer Officer

Chief Customer Officers are commonly accountable for the following outcomes:

1. Deliver operational and financial results for your company that contribute to growth in shareholder value. This increasingly includes owning a revenue and profit number.

2. Design and execute customer-facing experiences that generate adoption, usage, and expanded relationships with your company.

3. Advocate for the needs of your customers and your customer-facing teams to your company's executive leadership team and board of directors.

4. Manage a range of customer-facing functional teams that engage with your customers after they purchase your product, service, or solution.

5. Act as the cross-functional champion for internal initiatives that contribute to improved customer experiences and outcomes.

6. Balance the short-term needs for the delivery of current period results with the need to define and execute strategic priorities to improve and support scale and growth in the future.

One trend that has changed over the past few years is that the Chief Customer Officer now has a much wider span of control. This broader scope requires them to be effective organizational leaders and communicators. They are often responsible for a Profit and Loss Statement (P&L) that includes a potentially high percentage of the team members at their company. They also contribute directly to revenue and profitability growth.

CCOs need to allocate resources efficiently across all their teams. They also need to demonstrate an analytical understanding of the levers that drive financial results across each of their functional teams. They have accountability for board-level outcomes that significantly impact shareholder value. So they need to demonstrate strategic thinking and long-range planning to ensure that the results are repeatable and scalable as the company grows.

It is great to see that the CCO role is becoming more prevalent across such diverse industries, including financial services, healthcare, consumer packaged goods, business services, hospitality, and technology. Nestlé USA has a Chief Customer Officer whose scope of responsibility is a bit different from the Chief Customer Officer at UnitedHealth Group or American Airlines. For all of them, they are responsible for promoting a customer-centric mindset at their companies and improving experiences across all their customer interactions and channels.

The exact contours of the role may depend on the size of the company, the competitive environment, the capabilities of other members of the executive team, and the priorities and preferences of the CEO. However, there are a number of departments that commonly report to a Chief Customer Officer. In this chapter, you will learn about the high-level expectations and success metrics for each of these functional organizations. You will also get visibility into the strategic decisions that often confront leaders of these teams.

Who Does a Chief Customer Officer Report To?

In most cases, a Chief Customer Officer will sit on the CEO's executive staff and report directly to the CEO. With this level of visibility, CCOs provide a critical customer-facing perspective into the decisions made with their executive team. They can also leverage these executive-level interactions to drive and influence high-priority, cross-functional initiatives. By reporting to the CEO and sitting on their staff, it sends a loud message to customers and employees that the CCO and the stakeholders they represent have a direct voice at the executive table.

However, there are also situations where a Chief Customer Officer might report to another C-level executive such as a Chief Revenue Officer, Chief Operating Officer, or President of Worldwide Field Operations. There are several scenarios where this may be appropriate. First, the CEO may have too broad a span of control and wants to manage a smaller scope of direct reports. Second, the CEO may have a skillset or interest that is not conducive to providing functional or management guidance to the CCO. This sometimes occurs with highly technical or product-focused CEOs. Third, there may be a desire to create a tighter executive team under a single executive (not the CEO) focused exclusively on the Go-to-Market functions. These Go-to-Market functions often include Marketing, Sales, and the teams under the responsibility of a Chief Customer Officer.

Even in these situations where a Chief Customer Officer does not directly report to the CEO, I strongly recommend that CCOs should have a seat on the executive staff. The voice of your customer-facing organization needs to have a place in company-level discussions and decisions.

Functional Teams Under a Chief Customer Officer

Chief Customer Officers are commonly responsible for designing the organization structure under their span of control. There is no single organization structure that works for every company and in every situation. So when deciding on the appropriate structure, you need to consider the needs of your business, the leadership capabilities of your team, and the size of your company. The structure that is appropriate for a global, multinational company will not be the same for a startup or for a roll-up of acquisitions. Your org structure will also naturally change as your business grows and evolves, so you need to stay nimble and flexible.

This CCO role most commonly includes the following set of functional teams:

- Onboarding/Implementation/Professional Services
- Customer Success Management
- Support
- Customer Operations
- Account Management/Renewals
- Customer Education/Certification

Less often, the CCO role is also responsible for:

- Community
- Delivery Partner Management

Onboarding/Implementation/Professional Services

This organization is the team that creates the first impression for your customers after they have made a buying decision. Expectations can be high for how quickly your customers can start to benefit from your product or service. The team responsible for this step in the customer journey plays an important part in meeting those expectations. Depending on your company's needs, these functions may be revenue drivers or they may be cost-centers. They may provide solutions for new or existing customers. The experiences may be delivered through self-service capabilities, your company's team members, or partner resources.

The primary strategic value of this part of your organization is that it provides expert resources to assist your customers with the onboarding, implementation, and ongoing maintenance of your solution. You can offer best practice guidance and knowledge transfer so that customers can quickly recognize the value they expect from your product or service. This function also often creates resources and processes that can be used by various internal and external stakeholders to efficiently onboard customers.

ONBOARDING/IMPLEMENTATION/ PROFESSIONAL SERVICES SUCCESS METRICS

Customer Metrics

- Time to first value
- Customer NPS/CSAT
- Unit cost-to-serve customers

Internal Metrics

- Contribution margin
- Services bookings
- Services revenue

Input Metrics

- Attach rate of services
- Team member utilization
- Forecast accuracy

Strategic decisions the leader may need to make over time:

- What offerings or experiences should you make available to your customers?
- Should these offerings or experiences be free or are they fee-based?
- Should you have a separate team that specializes in offering these services?
- Should you leverage partners or subcontractors in your resourcing model?

- What type of delivery model should you offer? High touch? Self-Service? Hybrid?
- What skills and capabilities are required from your team members and partners?
- Should you have different offerings or experiences for different customer segments?
- How do you anticipate capacity needs so you have the appropriate resources?

Successful leaders of this function are able to work closely with their sales teams to anticipate demand for their services and have the right resources in place with the appropriate skills required. This enables you to efficiently and consistently work with your customers to move them through these early experiences with your company. You also align with your CEO or CFO regarding what outcomes are most important for you to achieve. At different times of your company's evolution, the goals may shift from an intense focus on doing whatever it takes for customers to complete their onboarding to an equally intense focus on managing a certain level of profitability for the business.

Customer Success Management

Effective leaders of the Success Management function are able to measurably demonstrate the impact of their team's work on the company's revenue and profitability. This often comes from delivering outcomes tied to customer retention, revenue growth within the accounts, and the customer's overall adoption and satisfaction with your product or service experience.

Success Management organizations typically provide resources to the existing customer base to ensure they are efficiently and consistently recognizing value. Customer Success Managers offer best-practice guidance and knowledge transfer to help your customers achieve the outcomes they expect from your solutions. They are also often responsible for increasing customer engagement with both your solutions as well as with your company's team members.

One of the most important activities for a Success Management team is to define an early warning system for customers who may be struggling or at risk of churning their relationship with your company. Your activities are intended to identify issues, diagnose the root cause, and take action so you can save these customers. Another important activity is to work with your customers to expand their use of your solutions across their teams, businesses, or geographies. This enables you to grow the relationship and drive higher revenue.

Many Success Management teams also have direct responsibility for the commercial aspects of the renewal process or the expansion of contractual relationships with customers. In these scenarios, the Customer Success Managers manage, negotiate, and complete the renewal or expansion transaction. In other companies, the renewal process or expansion process is managed by other functional teams such as a renewals team, an account management team, or a sales team. In these situations, the Success Management team is a contributor to this process but is not accountable.

TRENDS TO WATCH

Success Management teams are increasingly taking ownership of renewals and expansion sales.

I believe that these renewal and expansion responsibilities should reside somewhere in the Chief Customer Officer's organization. CCOs should have direct accountability for retention and expansion results. CCOs' teams are best positioned to understand your customer's experience with your product or service. And the CCOs are also best positioned to identify when customers can benefit from additional solutions available from your company.

When the teams are operating effectively, the Success Management organization is trained, skilled, engaged, informed, and trusted to achieve these outcomes. The reality though is that Success Management teams do not always have those skills and characteristics. In addition, company leaders may not be willing to put revenue growth at risk waiting for a developing Success Management leader to prove they can manage an expansion sales model or for a CSM team to demonstrate they can establish an accurate renewal forecast and contract management process. In many cases, the company executives defer to having one or both of these activities managed by a specialized team under a leader who has years of proven experience managing these functions.

However your company chooses to organize to optimize its renewal and expansion process, the CCO and its Success Management team should play a key role in achieving and measuring these outcomes. The CCO should actively seek increasing accountability for the commercial results of the business related to renewals and expansion.

Your success management team may be responsible for working with customers across all of your different product lines, geographies, and segments. The methods that you choose to interact with various groups of customers may differ based on their expectations and value to your business. Some groups may get a higher-touch experience, working directly with a success manager or a pool of success managers.

Others may get what is sometimes referred to as a "digital touch" or "automated experience." This could involve access to a series of email nurture campaigns, self-service training resources, webinars, and other highly leveraged communications. One evolving trend is for success management teams to work closely with your customer marketing organization. Customer marketers have a set of skills that can be very useful when developing personalized, high-impact communications at scale.

Success Management teams are also increasingly responsible for managing relationships with your company's partners. These partners may include technology integration partners, sales partners, or consulting delivery partners. These Success Managers are often segmented into a team called Partner Success.

TRENDS TO WATCH

More companies are creating Partner Success teams to manage relationships with third parties.

They play a similar role to ensure that these partners get the enablement, best practices, and ongoing support they need to provide high value to your company's clients. I believe this function of Partner Success is likely to become increasingly important to many companies over time. Keep an eye out for this trend.

CUSTOMER SUCCESS MANAGEMENT SUCCESS METRICS

Customer Metrics

- Product adoption
- Value recognition
- NPS/CSAT

Internal Metrics

- Net retention rate
- Gross retention rate
- Unit cost to serve

Input Metrics

- Ratio of clients per resource
- Account health
- Customer success qualified leads
- On-time renewal rate

Strategic decisions the leader may need to make over time:

- What should be the responsibilities and expectations for the team members?
- How will you measure success and the impact of your team on business results?
- Should your organization have accountability for revenue or commercial results?
- Which team should own the quota for renewals, upsells, or cross-sells?

- How should you segment to provide differentiated experiences to customers?
- How do you rationalize the investment in resources against the business goals?
- How often should customers leverage self-service or one -to-many resources?
- How to quantify your team members' contribution to retention or expansion?

Renewal Management/Account Management

The role of an Account Manager is slightly different from the role of a Customer Success Manager. They both have the same overall goals – to make sure that customers are satisfied with the experience using their product or service and that they grow their relationship with your company. But Account Managers most commonly have responsibility for completing renewal transactions, upsells, and cross-sells. They tend to focus more on the commercial aspects of the customer relationship and function more like quota-carrying salespeople.

As discussed in the previous section, Customer Success Managers often have responsibility for completing the renewal transaction. In other organizations, there may be a separate renewals team that works exclusively with customers on their renewal process. There are also scenarios where an Account Management team is responsible for all of the commercial transactions related to existing customers. The organization structure that is right for your business will depend on a number of factors including the complexity of the renewal process, the involvement of partners, the size of the customer, and the background of your functional leaders.

RENEWAL MANAGEMENT/ACCOUNT MANAGEMENT SUCCESS METRICS

Customer Metrics
- Product adoption
- Value recognition
- NPS/CSAT

Internal Metrics
- Net retention rate
- Gross retention rate

Input Metrics
- In-quarter renewal rate
- Percent of clients with two or more solutions
- Percent quota attainment

Strategic decisions the leader may need to make over time:

- What should be the responsibilities and expectations for the team members?
- How will you measure success and the impact of your team on business results?

- What incentive structure should you have in place to drive your desired outcomes?
- How will this team work with Customer Success Managers and the Sales organization?
- What segments of customers will have an Account Manager? A Renewals Manager?

Support

Successful support leaders are able to design an experience that allows your customers to quickly resolve their technical issues or get their product questions answered in a way that is scalable and cost-efficient. This organization can also be referred to as Customer Support, Product Support, Technical Support, or Customer Service. Whatever the naming convention, this team recognizes the importance of preventing the need to reach out for support in the first place. They put in place mechanisms to gather and prioritize feedback for the product team so they can address the underlying root cause of high-impact issues. Strong support leaders can effectively balance the need for fiscal efficiency in the support process with the desire to provide high-quality customer experiences.

Support teams provide resources to customers to help them resolve issues or get their product or service to function in the way that they expect. These capabilities can include self-service resources, automated chatbots, user community, as well as live chat, email, and phone support. One of the desired outcomes is to enable customers to quickly get back to using your solution successfully and not have to invest time troubleshooting or looking for answers. Interactions with a support organization are often the most common touch points with a company and can set the tone for how a customer feels about your solution. The support team can also be the front line for hearing about what customers like or don't like about new products and services your company introduces.

SUPPORT SUCCESS METRICS

Customer Metrics
- Resolution rate
- Time to resolve
- Service levels

Internal Metrics
- Cost per case
- Support costs as a percentage of revenue
- Case deflection rate

Input Metrics
- Staffing levels
- Resolution rate by channel
- Top case drivers

Strategic decisions the leader may need to make over time:

- What SLA (ie. response time) and resolution rate should you set for your team?
- What channels of support should you offer to your customers?
- How much time and money should you invest in self-service or one-to-many resources?
- Where should you staff your team members? Should they be internal or vendor resources?
- Should you offer differentiated levels of support for different customer segments?
- Should you offer fee-based premium support services for higher-value customers?
- How can you best work with your product teams to prevent the issues or questions in the first place?

Customer Education

Effective Customer Education leaders are able to leverage content created by different organizations to create a centralized, consolidated set of learning and training resources. This allows customers and partners with different learning needs to easily access the materials appropriate for them. Strong education leaders do this in a way that is efficient to deliver, easy to use, and financially scalable. Building out a successful education program can also significantly decrease the cost-of-service by reducing the need for customers to engage with higher cost team resources to learn common skills, techniques, and best practices.

Education teams offer training resources and learning paths that allow customers and partners to learn best practices and common techniques for using your products or services. They consolidate and organize this information from across the many different potential repositories so it can be easily accessed at the time it is needed.

Ideally, Education teams offer both instructions for how to use your product or service to achieve customers' desired outcomes as well as context regarding when your product or service can be used in different use cases. Many organizations also offer either formal certifications, informal badges, or other recognition programs to acknowledge the commitment of your customers and partners. This can be an effective way to build deeper relationships between your company and these stakeholders.

A growing number of companies offer fee-based training solutions. These offerings can include instructor-led training courses as well as subscriptions to higher-value self-service training content. This revenue can be important to offset the cost of the education team's resources.

In addition to being responsible for customer-facing training, many education organizations are also accountable for partner training as well as internal team member enablement. This is an evolving trend that you may want to keep in mind when considering the roles and responsibilities of your functional teams.

CUSTOMER EDUCATION SUCCESS METRICS

Customer Metrics

- Course completion rates
- Consumption of training resources
- Certifications passed

Internal Metrics

- Retention rate per trained customer
- P&L of the education function
- Number of customers trained
- Expansion revenue per trained customer
- Support cases deflected

Input Metrics

- Staffing levels
- Content development costs

Strategic decisions the leader may need to make over time:

- Who should be the target audience for your learning and training resources?
- What resources in your business will create the content? Who will organize that content?
- What personas should your content and learning paths be optimized for?
- Should you leverage partners or outside resources to create content or deliver training?
- What level of quality do customers expect from your education organization?
- What resources and budget should be invested in your education business?
- Should you charge fees for any training or education services?
- How will the team gather and prioritize ideas for new education content?
- What role, if any, will subject matter experts (SMEs) play in the creation of training content?

Customer Operations

Successful Customer Operations leaders are able to provide centralized expertise to the Chief Customer Officer's various customer-facing functions. This operational expertise enables these functional organizations to accurately, efficiently, and predictably deliver against their intended business outcomes.

Customer Operations teams often provide consistent access to the reporting, results, and insights that enable the various leaders to make informed decisions. They also commonly manage the evaluation, implementation, and maintenance of software solutions that support the various post-sale teams.

An increasing number of Customer Operations teams consolidate data into actionable reports and dashboards that can be easily accessed by other internal organizations. Some Customer Operations teams lead cross-functional initiatives that require the collaboration of resources across multiple teams. Other Customer Operations teams provide centralized resource management and capacity planning recommendations. This can include oversight of staffing decisions for your customer-facing resources as well as relationship management for partner delivery partner resources.

Customer Operations is a relatively new function. Its roles and responsibilities are quickly evolving. It is also a function that is navigating its place among the many different "operations" teams at a company – Marketing Operations, Sales Operations, Revenue Operations, Business Operations, Developer Operations. Chief Customer Officers and their post-sale teams absolutely need a specialized operations team and resources to support their needs. It is not clear yet whether this organization needs to report directly to a CCO or whether this function could report to another centralized operations leader and still achieve the same results.

CUSTOMER OPERATIONS SUCCESS METRICS

Systems and Tools
- Time to implement
- Internal user adoption rates

Reporting
- Forecast accuracy
- Reporting accuracy

Resource Management
- Resource utilization
- Internal vs. subcontractor resources

Strategic decisions the leader may need to make over time:

- What operational functions should be owned by the Customer Operations team?
- When should you start investing in a Customer Operations function?
- What results and expectations do you have for the team?
- What level of funding and resourcing is appropriate for this organization?

- How do you allocate and prioritize the team's time against its multiple priorities?
- What systems should the post-sale organizations invest in rolling out?
- What is the interaction model between this team and Revenue Operations, Marketing Operations, Business Operations, Sales Operations, and any other operations teams?

Titles Matter

At this point, you may be saying to yourself, "I have the set of responsibilities that you just described, but I don't have a Chief Customer Officer title." Maybe the peers on your executive team have C-level titles, and you are at a VP or SVP level. Perhaps your colleagues are getting promoted, and you aren't. I have spoken with countless leaders who are frustrated and disappointed that they consistently had titles that were lower than their peers.

Titles matter. They matter to your customers. They matter to your employees. They matter to you. Titles provide a certain clarity and set of expectations for how a leader can respond. They demonstrate a level of credibility, accountability, and decision-making authority. Your employees want to know that their functional leader is valued and has a seat at the table. Yes, there are situations where titles can be inflated and other times when they are undeserved. But there are plenty of situations where being promoted to a certain level in an organization is appropriate and deserved, and those promotions just aren't happening.

This book will help you accelerate your career path and provide you with actionable strategies. I cannot promise that you will get promoted or that your executive team will instantly recognize your value to the company. But I can assure you that you will be better positioned to move up the ladder and be successful as a Chief Customer Officer. You will also be better equipped to have a discussion with your manager about the criteria you together can use to evaluate your performance and readiness for an expanded role.

Compensation Matters Too

I would love to print the definitive study of what you can expect to earn as a Chief Customer Officer, SVP, or VP-level, customer-facing executive. The truth is that study is impossible to put together at this time. The minute a survey would be completed, it would be out of date. Plus, the survey wouldn't be able to take into account many relevant considerations including geography, company stage and size, years of experience and so many other factors.

What I can say is that the compensation model for post-sale leaders all the way up to the CCO role is very compelling. I work closely with a number of executive search firms that have practice areas that specialize in CCO and other post-sale executive searches. The recent trends around hiring and compensation practices are very encouraging.

Here are a few insights and trends they shared:

- Compensation packages for Chief Customer Officers have gone up significantly in the past few years, reflecting the demand for CCO roles and their impact on company valuation.
- Compensation packages regularly include base salary, bonus, and equity. In some cases, the variable component may be setup as a commission structure. Like other executive roles, equity compensation can be a material part of the compensation package.
- The percentage of bonus often depends on whether the CCO has revenue ownership. Owning a revenue number tends to lead to higher bonus opportunities.
- Chief Customer Officers often have higher base salaries than Chief Revenue Officers (CRO). But since CROs may have variable pay that can provide bonuses or commissions of up to 100% of their salary or more, their total cash compensation is commonly higher than CCOs. This reflects the risk/reward element of a CRO's success metrics.

- If a CCO has a track record of driving retention metrics up, they should be able to advocate for higher amounts of equity if retention is a significant driver of company valuation.
- CCOs should be comfortable tying their financial upside to Net Retention Rate and Gross Retention Rate growth. Everyone wins if those numbers increase.

At this point, you should better understand the scope of a Chief Customer Officer position. You have learned about different organizational functions that commonly report to the role. You have also learned about the expectations that CEOs and CFOs have for individuals in this role. In the next chapter, you will be introduced to a framework of eight skills and behaviors that CCOs and aspiring CCOs need to master to be successful in this role.

CHAPTER REVIEW

QUESTIONS TO CONSIDER

- What are the three to five most important responsibilities and expectations for your role?
- How is success measured for your current position?
- Do you have alignment with your CEO, CFO, and your manager on your goals and KPIs?
- Is your current organization structure optimally designed to support your ability to achieve your goals? Why or why not?
- Do your functional team leaders understand their responsibilities, expectations, and success metrics? If not, what actions can you take to clarify them?
- Do you believe you currently have the right title for your role and scope of responsibility?

ACTION PLAN

- Document your roles, responsibilities, expectations, and success metrics.
- Review this document with your manager, CEO, and CFO to get feedback and agreement.
- Document the roles, responsibilities, expectations, and success metrics for your managers.
- Review these documents with your functional peers to create shared understanding.
- Address any gray areas or gaps with your peers, leadership team, or executive team.

Part 2

The Path to Becoming a Chief Customer Officer

The Path to Becoming a CCO - The CCO Maturity Model™

During high school, I worked at my mother's dry-cleaning shop after school. I made it a game to remember each customer's name and something about them. When the customers came in to pick up their clothes, I greeted them each by name. I could already start to find the location of their clothes on the carousel that circled through our store. Our customers really appreciated that a local teenager cared enough to make their mundane trip to pick up their clothes a bit more pleasant and speedy than they might otherwise expect.

There, I learned how valuable it could be for a business to create personal relationships with its customers. I also found that I loved the challenge of finding ways to make a simple customer experience into a delightful one. This was the first step on my own journey to becoming a Chief Customer Officer.

Do you have your own origin story that helped you develop an interest in working with customers? I find that leaders who end up in customer-facing roles often have experiences early in life which introduce them to the value of going that extra mile.

Maybe you worked at an ice cream shop like Maranda Dziekonski, the CCO of Swiftly, which is the leading platform for transit agencies around the world. Maranda got immense pleasure from seeing the smile on a kid's face when she handed them their cones with sprinkles.

Perhaps you worked as a server at a restaurant like Christine Rimer, the CCO of the retirement plan software platform, Guideline. Christine was motivated by the connection between the experience you provided and the tip you earned. Christine even gamified her approach to maximizing tips, working hard to get her average nightly tips to increase as a percentage of the bill.

Kristi Faltorusso, CCO of customer success software platform, ClientSuccess, worked at an Italian bakery as a teenager and took immense pride that customers would come to the store every morning asking specifically for her to make them her perfect espresso cappuccino.

David Sakamoto, VP of Customer Success at the DevOps software platform, GitLab, was an intern at Silicon Graphics, where his colleagues were creating the tools that enabled the creation of the early Jurassic Park movies. He treated his colleagues like customers, listening closely to understand their expectations, and then following up to make sure he delivered what they needed.

Star Hofer, the CCO of the leading partner management software platform, PartnerStack, shared that her path to becoming a CCO started when she was a counselor at a camp for military cadets in Canada. She taught the new cadets to sail and use nautical equipment. She realized that she loved transferring knowledge to others and helping people grow their skills. Hofer also said that this was when she first recognized that she could be a great leader.

There is no single career path to becoming a Chief Customer Officer. Some CCOs started out as technical support agents or customer success managers or implementation consultants. Others kicked off their careers in sales or worked with a Big Five consulting firm. Some come from IT or operations team backgrounds. Throughout this book, you will hear stories from successful CCOs and you will learn about the diverse set of paths they each followed.

Sometimes their role progression was linear and spaced out as they transitioned from Manager to Director to Vice President to Chief Customer Officer. Other times the leaps to new roles were accelerated or unexpected as opportunities presented themselves and new challenges were accepted. You will map your own journey.

The skills and behaviors to become a Chief Customer Officer can be learned and perfected. This journey doesn't require any particular academic background or technical expertise. And this book helps you build upon the skills you already possess and explore new ones that are important for success in this role.

The Chief Customer Officer Maturity Model™

My research has identified a common set of eight skills and behaviors required to progress successfully in this type of customer-facing leadership role. These eight strategies form the framework outlined in the Chief Customer Officer Maturity Model™. Each chapter in this book shares stories, examples, and techniques to help you develop your skills in each of these eight areas. Once you are aware of these important skills, you will become better able to search for opportunities to practice and master them.

For each of these eight strategic skills, I also point out "career accelerators." These are opportunities or experiences that expose you to a new or uniquely challenging situation that may help you move along faster in your career. Remember the game Chutes and Ladders you may have played when you were a kid? These are sort of like those ladders. Not all the ladders may move you up the path that much more quickly. But they do keep you moving along in the right direction.

Certain skills will be appropriate for you when you are new to a role or if you are in an earlier part of your career. Other strategies may be more relevant for you to develop as you take on a broader role or become more senior at your compa-

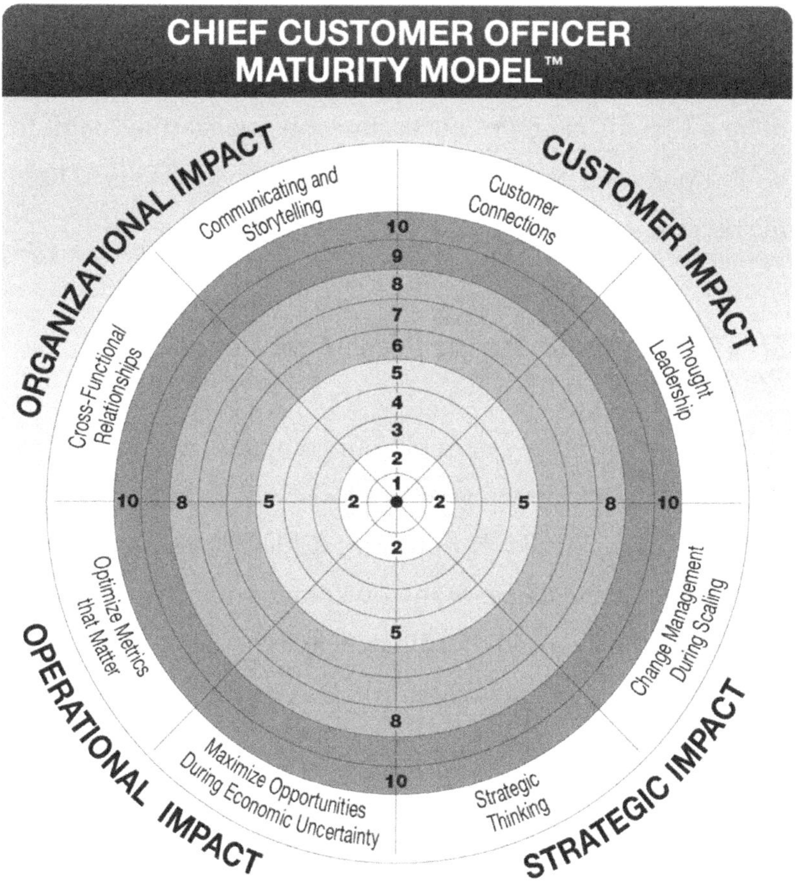

For each area in the CCO Maturity Model, rate yourself or have your manager rate you on a scale of 1-10 (1 being Manager level and 10 being CCO level).

You are operating at the level of a:

1-2 Manager **3-5** Director **6-8** VP **9-10** CCO

ny. For example, just because I created good relationships with my clients at the dry cleaners, it didn't make me ready to be a Chief Customer Officer. But it was a starting point to build upon a set of progressively more relevant skills to help me become a successful customer-facing executive.

Strategy 1: Build Strong Cross-Functional Relationships

As you become more senior at your company, you will notice that the results of your team's efforts will increasingly contribute to company-level outcomes. Chief Customer Officers face a unique challenge: Many outcomes you are responsible for delivering require coordinated activity across organizations outside your span of control. Driving these high-impact initiatives requires working cross-functionally to get things done through other people. Leading these cross-functional projects also creates an opportunity to leverage a growing network of industry peers in customer-facing roles that have faced similar opportunities and challenges. These cross-functional relationships and industry peer relationships can be an invaluable source of expertise, empathy, and collaboration. You will learn specific actions you can take to build your cross-functional network to help you deliver strong results and propel your career forward.

Strategy 2: Optimize Results from Metrics That Matter

To succeed as a Chief Customer Officer, you must build credibility with your CEO and CFO. C-level executives are counted on to deliver the expected financial results and customer outcomes. The executive team has a responsibility to shareholders to continuously increase the value of the organization. Whether you are responsible for all the customer-facing teams or just one or more of them, you will need to understand the levers to pull to continuously improve results. You will also need to understand how all the levers across your teams interact with each other to optimize performance across your areas of responsibility. You will be expected to do this with predictability and reliability.

Strategy 3: Establish Deep Customer Connections

Two of the most important roles you have as a CCO are to understand the critical needs of your customers and to then advocate for them. This comes through one-on-one interactions with certain customers and through the interpretation of customer needs through a variety of listening posts. There are three primary categories of customer-related skills for CCOs to develop and demonstrate. First, you need to build strong personal relationships with a number of key customer executives. Second, you should build a strong understanding of the needs of your key customers so you can empathize with their desires and expectations. Third, you can internalize this understanding so you can serve as an advocate for your customers in all corners of your company. This includes considering how the needs of your customers are integrated into your corporate culture. You will learn from several experts about how you can expand this capability to become an impactful customer champion.

Strategy 4: Communicate Effectively and Tell Stories

As a Chief Customer Officer, you will need to consistently demonstrate your ability to communicate the vision, strategies, and results of your organization's work to an increasingly broad set of stakeholders. These could include your executive team, customers, cross-functional peers, employees, partners, and your board of directors. These diverse audiences will look for signals from you to instill them with relevant information, direction, confidence, and the values of your customer-facing teams. You will need to talk at the appropriate level of detail for each audience while maintaining the ability to easily adjust your focus up or down as needed. Different audiences will also expect you to frame your communications around different time horizons. Sometimes your communications need to focus on today, this month, or this quarter. In other situations, such as communicating to your board, you will want to communicate about strategies that may go out through the fiscal year or even across multiple years.

Strategy 5: Demonstrate Strategic Thinking

As you progress in your career, you will need to demonstrate your ability to understand the longer-term needs of your business and put in place the appropriate people, processes, and technology required to grow. You may have opportunities to contribute to the strategic priorities of your company as part of the annual budgeting and planning process. You may need to develop quarterly goals and initiatives that sustain the continuous improvement required. You may also need to respond to more urgent strategic challenges that result from a customer situation, a team need, or a competitive threat. You will learn techniques to help you define and drive more impactful strategic initiatives that deliver measurable results for your company.

Strategy 6: Drive Change During Growth and Scaling

Your work as a post-sale executive is never complete. There are always opportunities to continuously improve processes, accelerate time to value, increase retention rates, or expand profitability. During times of fast growth, you will need to drive change that scales your operations effectively to deliver these improved results for your customers and business. You will learn techniques to effectively scale your organization during times of growth by applying the Post-Sale SCALING™ Framework.

Strategy 7: Maximize Opportunities During Economic Uncertainty

During difficult economic times, it becomes even more important for companies to hold onto their existing customers. Therefore, the role of the CCO also becomes more important. As your company's sales pipeline slows and it takes longer to bring in new customers, you can become an internal champion for the need to retain and grow your existing customer base. If you haven't gotten attention from your executive team in the past, you are likely to be in the spotlight moving forward. You will learn strategies that help you optimize performance during times when your company may not be growing or when the business is underperforming.

Strategy 8: Create and Share Thought Leadership

Chief Customer Officers are increasingly expected to be a source of expertise and best practices for your customers and employees. You are expected to have your company's clearest understanding of how the customer experiences interact to deliver value. This creates an opportunity for you to consolidate this expertise and share it as appropriate with your customers, employees, executives, prospects, and peers. You can demonstrate this value in many ways: writing, speaking, one-on-one discussions, events, conferences, and social media outlets. You can share observations, case studies, stories, mistakes, and best practices. The important takeaway is that you are sharing learning that is useful and engaging. You will read specific examples of how you can easily develop and impactfully share your experience with others.

Where Are You on the Chief Customer Officer Maturity Model™?

I developed this Chief Customer Officer Maturity Model™ framework to help you visualize the eight different skills and behaviors. The CCO Maturity Model™ is powerful because it gives you a visual representation of your current strengths and growth opportunities compared to the expectations for the different levels in a post-sale organization.

Using the Chief Customer Officer Maturity Model™ on page 65, you can rate yourself on a score of 1-10 for each of the eight areas. You could also do this exercise with your manager to see how they would rate you along these same competencies. This can be an excellent tool to get aligned on what it will take to move up in your company.

Throughout this book, you will learn about actions you can take to develop your skills so that you can make progress in each of these areas.

You can also visit www.ccoplaybook.com/resources where you can download the CCO Maturity Model™ worksheets.

CHAPTER REVIEW

QUESTIONS TO CONSIDER

- Where are you on your career path to be an effective and high-impact Chief Customer Officer?
- What are the skills and behaviors that you consider strengths?
- What input and help do you need from your manager to grow your career?
- What actions could you take to continue to enhance your strengths? To fill your gaps?
- Do you have a shared understanding with your manager about what results and expectations need to be met for you to be promoted? If not, what steps could you take to get aligned?

ACTION PLAN

- Rate yourself on a scale of 1-10 on each of the eight strategic skills in The CCO Maturity Model™. Identify areas where you have strengths. Identify areas where you have opportunities to grow.
- Ask your manager to rate you on a scale of 1-10 on each of the eight skills.
- Identify which of the eight skills where there are significant differences in how you rate yourself and how your manager rates you. Assess and discuss the gap. Use this as one input to identify and prioritize opportunities for you to work on areas that are important to your business.
- Get alignment on expectations for continuing to grow in your role and any promotion path.

Strategy 1
Build Strong Cross-Functional Relationships

Right after I joined Marketo, one of the first relationships I prioritized was with my Sales-leader counterpart. The company was struggling with churn, driven by what the executive team believed was poor onboarding and enablement of new clients. Before I started, the relationship between our sales and post-sale teams was confrontational and unproductive. The Sales team felt like the implementation teams just slowed down their deals and got in the way. And the implementation teams felt like sales teams just sent them junky customers whose expectations were not set correctly. Sound familiar?

I invested quickly and sincerely in changing that dynamic. My leadership team and I spent Fridays sitting on the sales floor to do our work so we could get to know the Sales team better. My Sales leader and I met weekly to review upcoming deals so we could collaborate more closely. I presented every month at the Sales all-hands meeting so the entire organization came to know me and my team personally. On the last day of every quarter, my team and I would buy treats and walk around the sales floor giving out ice cream sandwiches, caramel corn, or donuts. On New Year's Eve Day, I brought my kids into the office, and we gave noisemakers and hats to show our appreciation for the salespeople that were working and trying to close deals on the last day of the fiscal year.

The point was that I was making an active decision to invest in building strong relationships with important cross-functional partners. I wish I had time to meet every functional department and not just leaders but there is not enough time. You should evaluate which relationships are the most important. Then work thoughtfully to nurture them.

As you become more senior in an organization, there is an expectation that the results of your team's efforts will increasingly contribute to company-level outcomes. As the Chief Customer Officer, you may be accountable for improving retention rates, raising net promoter scores, driving product expansion, decreasing support costs, or increasing margins in your various teams. It is crazy to think that you can achieve these results with just the people in your organization. There are critical dependencies on other organizations that each have their own priorities and initiatives beyond what you need from them. Driving cross-functional teamwork is really hard, and that aspiration takes work. But you cannot achieve your goals without this collaboration.

Why Is It Important to Build Strong, Cross-Functional Relationships?

One of the challenges of being a Chief Customer Officer is that many of the improvements that your customers and employees need require multiple functions in your organization to work together. Improving new-customer onboarding can often benefit from enhancements to the product. Those changes require engagement from the product team. Decreasing support case volume often requires improvements to documentation, product functionality, and sometimes even expectation setting from Sales. Increasing retention rates likely involves an even broader set of cross-functional teams. Creating professional services or support offerings requires involvement from your marketing, sales, and finance teams. The list could go on and on. Initiating almost any impactful initiative requires working cross-functionally to get things done through others.

Maybe you look back on what you feel were the good old days. Perhaps you were an education leader and your teams could create training content and deliver courses with minimal involvement from other teams. Or perhaps your implementation teams could generally get customers up and running, even though you wished the process was a little easier. Now as a CCO, achieving your fundamental business goals is highly dependent on achieving effective cross-functional engagement with other teams.

I recently spoke to Sean Jacobsohn, who is a partner at Norwest Venture Partners, a venture capital and growth equity investment firm. He has been an investor and board member at a number of top technology companies for more than a decade. When I asked him about the most valuable characteristics he expects from Chief Customer Officers, his first answer was their ability to collaborate cross-functionally across their respective companies.

"Everyone at the company is involved in servicing the customer, even if they don't work for the CCO," Jacobsohn said. "The CCO needs to be able to leverage resources across the entire organization."

Given the dependency of your organization on working successfully with other functions, establishing a strong foundation of partnership, trust, and collaboration is critical for you as s leader. Relationships with your cross-functional peers should be proactively developed and nurtured. This does not mean that you should set up regular meetings with every single cross-functional leader at the company. You would never have time to get your work done. Nor would they.

PITFALLS

Avoid spreading yourself too thin. Focus on the high priority, cross-functional relationships.

What this type of relationship does mean is that you should identify and prioritize those peers where your time would be most valuable and impactful for you to establish a deeper relationship. Depending on transactional relationships to move the big rocks in your organization is risky, especially when you need to improve complex customer experiences or business outcomes. Don't wait until you are in a crisis to seek other leaders' input and advice. Make this feedback a regular part of your interactions. Your peers want to know that you value their experience and input, particularly in areas where there is a mutual dependency. These interactions are a show of respect and trust.

These relationships can also be mutually beneficial. Think about how much the product organization can benefit from learning what is actually happening in the market from your teams. Or how the sales team can better target customers if they understand the real-world impact of your solutions. You are on this journey together.

In his book, *The Speed of Trust,* Stephen M.R. Covey explains that the ability to build relationships with others is based on a foundation of trust. This trust leads to credibility and influence. Without trust, he shares that it is difficult to influence others and cooperate with them. He lays out four cores of trust: Integrity, Intent, Capabilities, and Results. You can use Covey's book as a resource if you want to dig more into the frameworks and best practices for building trust and relationships with others.

What Can You Do to Establish and Nurture Those Critical Relationships?

Prioritize the Most Important Functions and Relationships

For most of the post-sale executives I work with, I recommend that they focus on building particularly close relationships with leaders from four functional organizations: Sales, Product, Finance, and Marketing. These functions fit into the potential BFF (best friends forever) category. Their impact on your organization's results is consistently high and frequent. By prioritizing your investment of time on a small number of leaders, you give yourself a better opportunity to create those deep, mutually beneficial bonds.

Working closely with Sales, Product, and Marketing teams may seem obvious. Why Finance?

Chris Hicken is the CEO of the customer-led growth software platform, 'nuffsaid, and the past President and Chief Operating Officer of the publicly traded user experience research software platform, UserTesting. Hicken believes that successful CCOs must have a strong understanding of how the financials of their business work.

He comments that "Executives should understand the unit economics of their business, how gross profits are measured along with key metrics that investors look for. Core finance training is a huge miss for CCOs."

This is where developing a great relationship with your CFO or finance partner comes in. These finance partners tend to know what is going on around the company and can provide context to decisions that are made that could impact your organization. They are also experts in numbers and can help you to be smarter about your organization's results and the levers that drive change.

CAREER ACCELERATOR

Develop a collaborative relationship with your CFO or Finance Business Partner.

Understand and Acknowledge What's Important to Your Peers

One of the behaviors I find most entertaining about being part of an executive team is that each functional leader absolutely believes that they have the hardest job at the company. Those of us in post-sale leadership roles may definitively know that our role is ACTUALLY the hardest (wink, wink), but it is still possible to gracefully acknowledge that other leaders may have challenging jobs too.

To build those mutually beneficial relationships, understanding what is important to your peers and to have context for how their performance is measured is helpful. This can be incredibly beneficial when trying to anticipate how they prioritize their work and how they might respond to requests from you or your organization. Take time to learn about their goals, success metrics, and Key Performance Indicators (KPIs). This also provides context for finding areas where your interests align or potentially conflict.

The best way to develop this awareness is to ask questions. This task seems simple but is frequently overlooked. Listen closely to your peers to learn about their priorities for the year, and also how those priorities might be changing based on what is happening this month or this quarter. Seek to understand their challenges and constraints. You can also listen for ways that you and your organization can help them achieve their goals. They will appreciate your interest in their team and your sincere awareness of the ways that you can support them.

When your role or title changes at your company, that can be a great time to re-establish these relationships in the context of your new responsibilities or position. Even though you may already know that person, it can be helpful to do a "listening tour" to reset expectations for how you and your peers can work together toward common company goals. Re-establishing expectations also gives you an opportunity to demonstrate that you can bring a higher level of awareness to your organization.

Here are a few ways to start that discussion. For example, you can start with, "I am trying to better understand how our organization can support your team."

Then you can ask:

- Would you mind sharing your team's goals and how your success is measured?
- What are your priorities for the next quarter/year, and what do you need from my teams?
- How is your team compensated so that we encourage behaviors to maximize their pay?
- What are the challenges your team faces that my teams could help influence?
- How could our teams work better together to help you achieve your goals?

Show Empathy for the Challenges of Your Peers

When I worked at RingCentral, I would travel regularly to the Philippines where we had hundreds of sales, support, implementation, and operations team members. Since I was already traveling those thousands of miles, I would take time to get to know the managers and team members in the other functional organizations. I understood that I was not just visiting as the customer-facing executive. I was representing the entire executive team of RingCentral from company headquarters.

CAREER ACCELERATOR

You are an ambassador for your executive team when visiting other locations and offices.

My executive peers from RingCentral's Sales, Operations, and Marketing functions appreciated that I was investing time to meet their team members, learn about their work and challenges, and understand how they contributed to the company's success. Showing this sincere interest in the team members of other functions also demonstrated to the broader organization that our executives operated with a "one-team" mindset.

This interest also humanizes your company's employees. They go from being "the support rep" or "the sales account executive" to being someone with a name that you know, who is just trying to do the best work they can for a company with a headquarters halfway around the world. When you get to know the managers and team members of other functions, you come to really appreciate how much effort they put into the work they do.

Being a leader isn't easy in any functional team at a fast-growing company. There is inevitably a combination of resource constraints, operational barriers, timing expectations, and execution challenges. By developing this mutual empathy, you will find yourself being more open to finding ways to collaborate to help each other out.

Mary Poppen is the CCO at involve.ai, a leading customer intelligence software platform, and the past CCO at LinkedIn and SAP. She described a "help me help you" mindset that she often uses with her executive-level peers to demonstrate empathy for the challenges that their teams face.

"I ask what else my team can be doing to help their team be successful," says Poppen. "Listening closely is huge because that is where you uncover some of the gaps that you may not even have been aware of. If you don't have those conversations, you can't get aligned and proactively stay ahead of obstacles."

Communicate Effectively and Consistently

During my time at Marketo, I would take every opportunity possible to get in front of the Sales team. I worked closely with Nadia Rashid, our VP of Sales at the time, who led the team in our newly opened Atlanta office. Every visit, I would engage actively with her organization. Sometimes, I would share the priorities and results of my functions. Other times, I would lead a town hall format or a small group meeting with a particular team. What these all had in common was a sincere desire to have clear, consistent communication about how important it was that the sales and post-sale teams worked together for the benefit of our customers.

As a result of these types of conversations, the Sales team members increased their engagement with their post-sale counterparts to get their support for closing deals. They were also quicker to provide feedback to our leadership team about how the teams could collaborate more effectively and without pointing fingers. After just a few quarters, the new Atlanta office was outperforming the more tenured San Francisco area office in sales results and team productivity. We all felt great about how the Atlanta team ramped so quickly.

Another communication tip I have found useful is to repeat important information. That's because people need to hear things multiple times for that new information to stick. That is why effective politicians have stump speeches and impactful CEOs reinforce company priorities and values again and again. New employees are constantly joining your company and they haven't heard from you before. Cross-functional team members might have missed a previous all-hands or internal training session. Or maybe they were multi-tasking during your last interaction with their team and didn't digest your message.

There are a number of other ways to communicate your priorities, results, and expectations with other teams:

- Volunteer to present at the staff meetings or all-hands for your peers.
- Walk the floor in your offices and get to know the influencers on those teams.
- Present at company all-hands meetings.
- Set up regular one-on-ones with peer leaders.

- Co-present with your peers about how your priorities align with each other.
- Seek advice and input from your functional peers on strategic issues.
- Create a presentation that shares your team's goals, priorities, and success metrics.
- Share these goals, priorities, and success metrics in a "roadshow."
- Set expectations for the type of interactions and handoffs you want from other teams.

CAREER ACCELERATOR

Regularly communicate your strategies and priorities to your stakeholders.

As you take on increasingly senior leadership roles, your ability to communicate successfully on behalf of your organization becomes even more important.

In a hybrid work environment where some individuals may be in the office and others remote, building your skill around communicating effectively becomes even more important. You may need to be more proactive to create opportunities to get your message across to your executive team, peers, and team members. You may need to find creative ways to keep people engaged when communicating your priorities and results. I also encourage you to find ways to be face-to-face whenever possible to establish those personal bonds that are more challenging to create in a virtual, remote environment.

Know Your Position on the Team and Play It Well

As a CCO, your first priority should be to understand the outcomes expected from your organization and then be transparent about working toward those goals. The outcomes expected by your CEO and CFO can sometimes be obvious, but that is not always the case. Yes, your implementation team is responsible for getting your new customers up and running quickly. Yes, your support team is responsible for resolving support issues efficiently.

But perhaps over the next quarter or two, your CFO needs your team to improve the profitability of your professional services business because the company wants to position itself better for an upcoming financing event. Perhaps you should be considering building out a partner consulting delivery channel, a new set of fee-based implementation offerings, or managing your teams to higher levels of consulting team utilization.

Maybe your teams need to provide feedback to the product team related to the launch of new solutions and features that are critical to future growth. Your organization works more closely with customers than any other team at the company. They are likely at the front line in hearing feedback about what's working, what's not working, and what customers would like to see improved. Your team could be in the best position to provide prioritized recommendations back to your product teams.

The takeaway here is to periodically align with your CEO and CFO so you can be confident that you understand what the company expects from you and your team.

Share Your Goals and Outcomes

It can be extremely valuable for you to communicate those outcomes and goals to your peers so they understand your context and situation. This communication also helps them understand the rationale for decisions that might impact them. If your communication is clear at a company level that your organization needs to improve profit margins for services, it will make more sense when you frequently push back on requests from sales for discounts on your implementation offerings. Make sure that you are communicating clearly to your organization and to your cross-functional peers about your business goals and priorities. Each cross-functional executive should have a clear understanding of the role that you play on your company's executive team.

The overall success of the company depends on each of the functional leaders delivering their goals and working together on joint initiatives. It is easier for executives to collaborate and invest their resources to support other organizations when they feel like their peers are all pulling their weight.

CHAPTER REVIEW

QUESTIONS TO CONSIDER

- Who are the most important peer leaders for you to build strong relationships?
- How would you describe the quality of the relationship between you and these peers?
- What could you be doing to enhance the collaboration between organizations?
- What outcomes are expected from you and your peers by your executive team?

ACTION PLAN

- Prioritize two to three functional organizations that require the most collaboration with you and your teams.
- Identify what you need from these functional peers and what you can offer them in return.
- Set up meetings to share your goals with those peers and seek to understand their needs.
- Create an opportunity to present to their leaders or functional organizations.
- Set up one new ongoing operating mechanism to maintain engagement and collaboration.

Strategy 2
Optimize Results from Metrics that Matter

Legendary Venture Capitalist, John Doerr, popularized a management methodology that used a goal-setting system of Objectives and Key Results (OKRs) that had initially been introduced by Intel's CEO, Andy Grove. In 2017, Doerr shared this approach in a book called *Measure What Matters*. Clearly defining your goals and sharing them with your organization helps create alignment that is critical for success. In this chapter, you will learn about a few of the most important metrics that drive top-line and bottom-line results in your part of the business.

As a CCO, you should be directly responsible for the achievement of company-level results. These results most commonly relate to increasing revenue growth and profitability. These are the fundamental growth engines of a company for driving increased shareholder value. In order to optimize your contribution to revenue and profitability growth, you need to become an expert at managing the people, processes, systems, and experiences that contribute to these outcomes.

CAREER ACCELERATOR

Take accountability for owning a revenue or profitability number whenever possible.

Know Your Numbers and How They Impact the Company

Becoming a successful Chief Customer Officer requires an evolution of your thinking about how you achieve results. Maranda Dziekonski is the CCO at Swiftly, a leading platform for transit agencies around the world. She observed that as a CCO, your thinking needs to expand beyond your team.

"It's not just about Customer Success. It's about your business success," she said. "You aren't running an organization. You are contributing to company outcomes."

Dziekonski said that one of her most valuable career accelerators was understanding her company's overall business metrics and operating levers.

"You have to have a curiosity to dig in and understand how to read a P&L. How do we do budgeting? How do I build a business case to be able to get more budget?" As a CCO, she competes with heads of Sales, Marketing, Product, and other departments for investment. She needs to be able to make a compelling case for why to invest in her functional teams over other alternatives for investing scarce capital.

I heard a similar message about knowing your numbers from several other CCOs I talked to as I wrote this book. Christine Rimer, the CCO of retirement plan software platform, Guideline, shared advice for aspiring CCOs that they should get very comfortable understanding their own functional metrics and their impact on the broader company financials.

"It is a role where you need to be data-driven," she said. She needs to understand the financial impact of conversion rates, headcount, burn rates, spending, and NPS investments. "You should be educating your CEO on how they should measure you."

Kristi Faltorusso, the CCO of customer success software platform, ClientSuccess, shared advice for aspiring CCOs that they should practice telling stories using the results from their business.

"I had to get really comfortable understanding how to use data to tell stories and how to find your story in data. I have all this information, but what is it telling me?" Faltorusso believes that it is critical for post-sale leaders to be able to use data to defend their decisions and to be able to explain their business results at the board level.

As a customer-facing executive, you may be asking yourself why you should care about the company's financial results. Shouldn't you just be focused on delivering the best possible customer experience? Yes, sort of. There can often be a sense of diminishing returns when it comes to investing in improving customer experiences. At some point, the additional investment required to make the experience marginally better doesn't translate into results that make much difference to the customer or to the company's results. Customers will feel about the same amount of happiness, their retention rates will stay the same, and their behavior won't differ very much.

As you move up the career path ladder, you will need to develop a more intuitive feel for the business results needed by your organization and the most important levers that drive those particular outcomes. You can also become better at quickly testing different approaches to see which ones move the needle the most on the outcome metrics you are trying to impact.

If you work at a publicly traded company, there is an additional aspect that requires consideration. I spoke recently with David Sakamoto who is the VP of Customer Success at Gitlab, a company that makes an industry-leading DevOps software platform. As a public company, you also have to manage to a certain level of predictability.

"If you are a public company, you are assumed to be at a certain level of scale. You need to have a mature discipline around your numbers and around forecasting," he said. Sakamoto also mentioned that as companies get larger, they often have more business units and product lines, adding to the complexity of coordinating activities across functions.

Output Metrics and Input Metrics for Your Company

Let me take a minute to explain output metrics and input metrics. During a few of the years I worked at Intuit, Steve Bennett was our CEO. Bennett had previously been a top executive at General Electric. One of the frameworks I remember was his explanation of the difference between *Input* and *Output* metrics.

Your *Output* metric is a function of various *Input* metrics. Plus there might be many different input metrics. These inputs are often behaviors or leading indicators. The insight is that not all of the input metrics have the same impact on driving results for the outcome metric you are trying to optimize. So you have to figure out which input metrics (behaviors, processes, leading indicators) contribute most directly to achieving the output metrics (results) that you expect.

For example, an output metric you may care about could be your Gross Retention Rate. Input metrics that may impact your Gross Retention Rate could be the frequency of product usage, the customer's account health, pricing compared to competitors, the engagement of an executive sponsor, or how long it took to start to see value from your solution. As a CCO, you may be ultimately accountable for optimizing the Gross Retention Rate, the output metric. You then have to decide how to allocate resources and investments to manage the input metrics to get the desired outcomes.

Let's take a look at what I call the CCO's Big 5 metrics that move the needle on company growth and profitability. Your company's Big 5 may differ based on the products and services you sell, but you can use these as a starting point. Depending on how your business is organized, you may want to look at company level metrics as well as results by customer segment, product, geography, or business unit.

Top Tier Output Metrics to Drive Revenue Growth and Profitability

#1 - Net Retention Rate

Net Retention Rate (NRR) has recently become the "Captain of the Metrics All-Star team" type of KPI, particularly for recurring revenue businesses. It is a metric that demonstrates how well your company is not only retaining its existing customers but also how well it generates additional revenue streams from that same group of existing customers. Jason Lemkin is the CEO of SaaStr, the world's largest community of SaaS executives, founders, and entrepreneurs. He has described high NRR as the "key to the magic in SaaS" and "the engine that lasts decades and fuels growth to far bigger levels."

To accelerate growth in top-line revenue, your company needs to continue to generate revenue from its existing customers while at the same time expanding its customer base by attracting new customers. Typically a company's marketing and sales organization are primarily responsible for attracting new customers. Your post-sale teams heavily contribute to being able to retain and grow your existing customers. The most successful CCOs and post-sale leaders are able to measure NRR, continuously improve this metric, and then tie the work their teams do to the results they achieve. They also have a deep understanding of the levers that have the biggest impact on NRR.

This metric is also important because your results can be benchmarked against NRR for your competitors and companies in other similar industries. Its recent popularity has increased the visibility of NRR as a key performance indicator of company-level results. Net Retention Rates can exceed 100%. The Software Equity Group has done research tracking a selection of public companies to demonstrate the positive correlation between net retention and the Enterprise Value/Revenue ratio. They say that their data proves that companies that are able to retain and grow with its existing customers are rewarded with higher multiples of shareholder value.

ICONIQ Growth recently published its annual *Topline Growth and Operational Efficiency* report that benchmarked more than 100 of its portfolio companies and high-performing public companies. Their analysis shows that the Top Quartile of performers had between 125-130% NRR. To see the ICONIQ Growth, visit www.ccoplaybook.com/resources

METRICS THAT MATTER

NRR is a measure of how effectively you retain and grow revenue from your existing customers.

#2 - Gross Retention Rate

Gross Retention Rate is often right behind Net Retention as a signal of how well your company is performing at delivering value for its customers. While Net Retention includes a measure of how existing customers stay with you and also upsell to expand revenue with you, Gross Retention focuses only on the retention side of the equation. It considers customers that leave your business entirely and also those that downsell over a given period of time. Because you are measuring how much of the customer's revenue still remains after a certain period of time, gross retention rates have a maximum of 100%.

Regardless of whether your organization is directly responsible for the renewal transaction or whether your work only contributes to retention, the work your team delivers across the customer lifecycle significantly impacts whether your customers choose to stay with your solution over time. That work could include how your team enables new customers, supports them throughout their lifecycle or delivers value through any in-person, automated, or self-service resources under your area of responsibility. Your teams should be measuring drivers of churn to understand why customers decide to leave. That gives your team data to inform where you invest time and resources to improve.

There may also be retention drivers that are part of your company's experience but that are outside your direct control. That includes inputs like product ease of use, price changes, and how well expectations were set in the sales process. Also, many conditions that influence a customer's propensity to stay with you may even be outside your company's control. That could include their own company health, turnover in their leadership team, changes in business strategy, and external economic factors.

ICONIQ Growth's benchmarking report showed that median annual churn rates were between 8-10% across companies with different cohorts of Annual Recurring Revenue. To see the ICONIQ Growth report, visit www.ccoplaybook.com/resources.

METRICS THAT MATTER

GRR is a measure of how effectively you retain revenue from customers compared to the start of the period.

#3 - Time to First Value for New Customers

Think of a time when you have signed up for a service and you could start using it right away. Maybe you recently signed up for a new television streaming service and you could instantly begin to watch your favorite movies. Or perhaps you purchased LinkedIn Premium so you can access a broader set of resources to help you find a new job.

What makes that situation so satisfying? There is an expectation in these situations that right after purchasing the service, it will be so easy to use that you can begin to receive the value you expected – you can watch your movie or search job listings. Time to first value is extremely short and can create a delightful first impression when the product or service works well.

Note that you, as a new user of services, may not initially be watching all the channels on your streaming service or using all the bells and whistles that come with your LinkedIn Premium subscription. But you were able to *start* using the service. That is why it would be described as *time-to-first-value*.

Time-to-first-value is often defined as the duration between when the customer purchases or signs up for the service and when they first start to be able to use it or receive some value from it. This could be measured in minutes, days, weeks, or months.

At some companies, the *time-to-first-value* can take weeks or months, especially if the solution is complex or requires company-wide rollout and training. Many business-to-business software applications require an implementation process that can take a surprisingly long time. Sometimes it requires the creation of an implementation project team to define requirements, build the integrations, and then design the workflow of how this new solution will work at your company. Then there may be the rollout training and change management.

In the past, many companies structured their implementation process so that there would be a big-bang release where the solution is not released for use until all the capabilities are ready. Increasingly, companies are moving to scenarios where certain use cases can be introduced more quickly, and then additional capabilities are added over time. This shortens the time-to-first-value.

Anita Toth calls herself the "Chief Churn Crusher." She runs her own customer insights research firm and helps her clients design better experiences that make their customers more loyal. She said that one of the most important reasons to accelerate time-to-value is to minimize the amount of time when customers might have "buyer's remorse."

"Time-to-first-value is one of those critical points where you want to quickly get them out of the trough where they might feel that onboarding is complicated and is taking too long," Toth says. "The implementation if not managed well can start planting the seeds of doubt. If that first time-to-value is too long, the seeds of churn can be planted." She observes that many times buyers have stuck their necks out to make an expensive purchase. "We often forget that there is an emotional journey underpinning all of this. It is not always a logical journey."

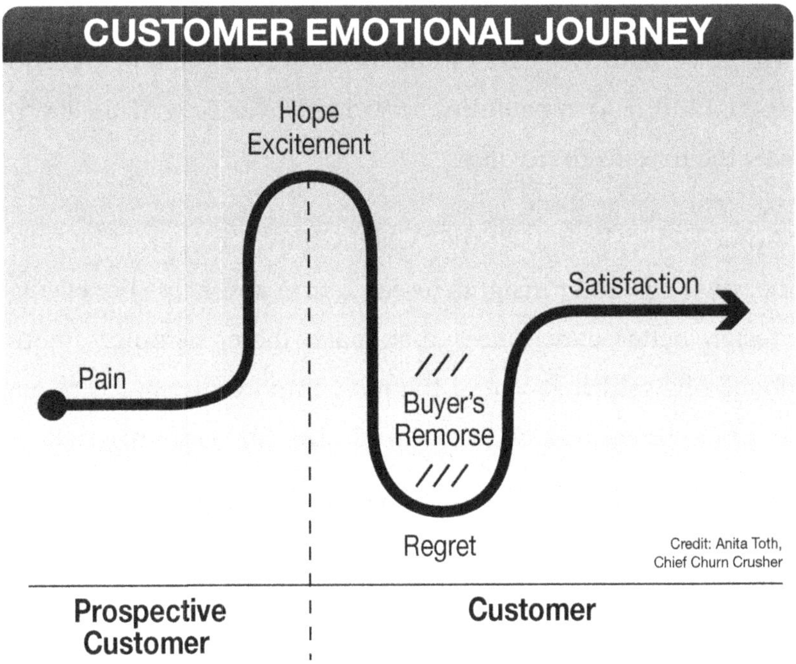

Whatever the duration of your *time-to-first-value,* you should measure it consistently and ensure that it is meeting the expectations of your customers. Sometimes, you can put in place processes to decrease the *time-to-first-value*. Other times, you can at least set expectations appropriately so that customers do not get surprised with the time it does take. It can also create situations where your company can start recognizing the revenue from the sale more quickly. In either case, accelerating time-to-first-value commonly has a direct impact on revenue growth.

METRICS THAT MATTER

Time-to-First-Value is a measure of how quickly your customers can start using your solution to achieve their goals.

#4 - Usage and Adoption of Your Product or Service

One of the most important factors for why customers continue to purchase your product or service is that they are using it and getting value from it. If you use your Peloton stationary bike regularly, you are likely to stay a member of their service. But if you don't use your bike after a few months, you are more likely to cancel your monthly subscription and start using the bike as a clothing rack. If you use Zoom all the time, you are likely to push back on your IT admins if they say they are thinking of turning Zoom off to move to a competitive service.

There are three metrics to consider when evaluating how to measure usage and adoption. First, you can look at the *frequency* that your customers are using your solution. Are they using the solution every day? Once a week? Infrequently? Never? Being able to track these metrics will give you a good sense of whether they are seeing the value they expected. Second, you can look at the *depth* of usage. Are they taking advantage of the basic capabilities? More advanced capabilities? Are the capabilities they are using the ones that will create "stickiness" with your product or service? Third, you can look at the *penetration rates* of your solution into their organization. If you sold 100 licenses, how many of them are actually being used?

Over the past few years, a number of solution providers have sprung up to make it easier for companies to track customer usage. This tracking can occur through mobile devices, on websites, in applications, or even through in-person interactions. For a list of recommended tech stack solutions, visit www.ccoplaybook.com/resources.

#5 - Unit Cost-of-Delivery

At the highest level, the cost-of-delivery (also known as cost-to-service) relates to the total cost of the resources to deliver your post-sale experiences as a percentage of the revenue generated from these customers. These costs could include labor costs for your team members or contractors, technology costs for the systems that support your team members, and other expenses and allocations absorbed by your organization. For software companies, this could include implementation, product support, success management, training, and other functional teams. This can be calculated on a dollar basis or as a percentage of revenue.

What starts to get particularly interesting is when you can also analyze your delivery costs by customer segment or product line. When I worked at Marketo, we looked at the profitability of customers in certain customer segments. We found that while our small business customers made up a large percentage of our customer logos, they were much less profitable to serve when compared to larger enterprise clients. The revenue we received from smaller customers was low. They tended to need a large amount of hand-holding during the implementation process. They contacted our support team frequently and their lifetime value tended to be lower because they churned more often than our larger clients.

Having a relatively high cost of delivery may not necessarily be a bad thing. The situation just depends on the goals of your company and the stage of growth that the company is in. For companies that are trying to grow the absolute number of customers or generate a network of advocates in the market for their solution, accepting a relatively high cost of delivery compared to the revenue received can be the right decision. For companies focused on improving profitability, there may be certain other actions that one would take based on a cost-of-delivery analysis.

METRICS THAT MATTER

Measure your unit cost to service and support your different segments to understand the impact on profitability.

Sridhar Gollapalli is the VP of Customer Success at Gainsight, the leading customer success software platform. He is responsible for leading the India-based team members in the Professional Services, Support, Customer Success, and Customer Operations teams. As Gainsight grew over the years and expanded its base of both commercial and enterprise clients, the company needed to find ways to more closely match the cost of its operating model to the revenues from its customer segments. Gollapalli has grown his team over the past six years from ten team members to over 200 people, delivering exceptionally high-quality experiences while taking advantage of lower-cost geographies.

"We were able to build a team that could deliver a high quality of service. The targets for the US team and the India team are exactly the same. Just because the team comes at a lower cost doesn't mean that it is lower quality. We can maintain the quality by adding people that are more mature and senior," Gollapalli said. This type of mindset, leadership, and operational execution has enabled Gainsight to scale its revenue while improving its operational efficiency and cost-to-deliver.

The most important takeaway from this section is that you need to understand your company's business model and that you should be measuring your results consistently. Talk to your CFO or finance business partner to make sure you understand your metrics and to help you perform the analysis. It is often called a unit-cost analysis. They will also likely be impressed that you are proactively thinking about this analysis. Understanding your cost of delivery is a tremendous motivator for improving the impact of your organization on business profitability. You also want to be focused on delivering these results in a consistent, predictable, and forecastable manner.

CHAPTER REVIEW

QUESTIONS TO CONSIDER

- What are the most important outcome metrics expected from your organization?
- Do you have alignment with your executive team on the targets to achieve?
- How well are you able to measure current period results and forecast future results?
- What levers do you have to improve results in areas where improvement is required?

ACTION PLAN

- Define the three to five most important metrics for your organization.
- Create two new reports or dashboards to show ongoing performance against those metrics.
- Align with your leadership and CFO on desired outcomes and any improvement opportunities.
- Identify one to two areas where you can work with or learn from your CFO or Finance business partner.
- Maintain visibility for you, your peers, and your executive team on current and forecasted results.

Strategy 3
Establish Deep Customer Connections

Recently I asked Justin Sadrian, a Managing Director at Warburg Pincus (a global private equity firm that focuses on growth-oriented investments), about the characteristics of successful Chief Customer Officers. Justin works closely with many of the firm's 75 portfolio companies that operate across the technology industry.

"A great Chief Customer Officer brings tremendous customer awareness. They work well with their clients, demonstrate consistent engagement, and dig deep to help them solve their business problems," he said. CCOs also need to have "thick skin" to work through client challenges calmly and professionally.

This sentiment is common among executives I have worked with. While Chief Customer Officers are expected to be capable executives that deliver consistently strong results, the special sauce that unites these particular leaders is their interest and ability to deeply connect with the needs of their customers. Nowhere else in an organization is this responsibility as critical to the fundamental success of their role.

What Does It Mean to Build Relationships With Your Customers?

As you grow in your career as a customer-facing leader, there are a number of skills that you can practice and develop. We will talk about a few of these skills in this chapter. However, I also believe that a number of core capabilities are more fundamental. For example, you have to enjoy interacting directly with customers. Not everyone enjoys that type of engagement. You need to have a bit of thick skin because interactions with customers are not always positive (that may be an understatement!). You are frequently called upon to resolve escalations without getting defensive and taking things personally. You also need to be the type of person that feels comfortable driving continuous improvement. Your team's work is never done. There are always things that can be made better or more efficient.

You can practice many of these skills, but if you fundamentally don't like interacting with customers, managing through difficult situations, or continuously working to make things better, then this career path may not be for you.

There are three primary categories of customer-related skills and behaviors that we will discuss in this chapter:

1. Building strong personal relationships with key customers
2. Understanding the needs of your customers
3. Being a champion for your customers inside your organization

Building Strong Personal Relationships With Customers

It might be impossible for a customer-facing executive to personally know all of your customers. Also, getting to know all your customers probably is not the best use of your time. However, as you progress in your career, nurturing your relationships with executives at key customers is imperative and can provide you with deeper insight into the experience they have with your product or service. The development of these trusted relationships can provide you with honest feedback and insight – good or bad. They also enable you to provide a window into your own organization for your customers.

So, how can you get started?

Make Connections With Leaders That Come in Through Escalations

While this might not be the most enjoyable part of your job, it actually can be a great way to identify senior executives who care enough about your product or service to engage with your team to resolve an important issue. This part of your job gives you an opportunity to show empathy for their situation. And your empathy can create an opportunity to better understand how your solution contributes to the operations of their business. This interaction can also cement trust if you are able to leverage your experience and leadership to turn around a challenging situation.

I remember having a discussion with Greg Higham, who is the CIO at a large and influential network management software company, Malwarebytes. The company was considering implementing a new software solution for one of its functional teams. Early on, Greg had expressed concern to me about the risk of potential delays in getting their software solution configured and implemented. Well, who wants their implementation to take longer than necessary?

The situation created an opportunity for the customer-facing executive working with Greg's team to make a personal connection with Greg to better understand his concerns. In particular, Greg's team had a calendar-driven window in which his IT organization could invest time in setting up this new software solution. Missing that window would have a negative impact on a number of other company-wide initiatives that Greg's team was leading. After buying the solution, the software vendor quickly set up the implementation project, accelerated the timeline, and provided executive-level project updates on a weekly basis. This helped Malwarebytes implement its solution in record time.

Working with an executive client through an escalation enables you to demonstrate that you understand their expectations clearly and that you can guide your team to ensure that you address those concerns. It also creates an opportunity for you to develop a communication cadence with this leader to provide them with updates about status.

Proactively Identify Key Customers and Build Relationships With Their Executives

You might want to develop direct relationships with your customer's executives. These may be large customers that generate high revenue. They may be strategic accounts that represent brands that you want to be able to associate with your company. They may be companies that have influential leaders that can provide you with particularly relevant insight about your solution. Or they might be customers using new products or solutions that can offer you early feedback about their experiences.

Building rapport with these leaders provides you with several benefits. First, these relationships give you first-hand insight into your customers' experiences which are important for your company's long-term success. These often turn into compelling stories that you can leverage in your interactions with internal teams. Second, these interactions enable you to synthesize data from this set of listening posts to provide input to your product, sales, and marketing peers. Being able to refer back to actual discussions with representative customers adds credibility to your message. Third, building relationships establishes mutual trust between you and those executives. They will feel more comfortable providing you with timely, honest feedback – good or bad – about their experiences. This enables you and your team to get early warnings without them turning into escalations to your CEO or other executives. Having these relationships also creates an opportunity for you to develop channels to get your own proactive input when you need to gather information quickly about a particular topic.

CAREER ACCELERATOR

> Build relationships with executives at key clients in each of your important customer segments.

As you progress toward a CCO level, you are also often expected to benefit from the value of your past relationships when you join a new company. These individuals may be prospects or customers of your new company. They may help you understand new industry areas or functional departments. They also may be a source of candidates as you hire and grow your future organization.

Create and Participate in a Customer Advisory Board

Many companies arrange for a set of customers to meet on an ongoing basis to provide guidance and insight to their organization. Participants on a Customer Advisory Board are often senior-level executives that can provide relevant insight into industry trends, company expectations, and competitive risks. These activities also give customers an opportunity to meet and interact with peers who often are themselves thought leaders and industry influencers.

There are various ways to execute a Customer Advisory Board Program. These programs can include in-person events, executive offsites, or regularly scheduled virtual meetings. They can also be organized by different functional departments at a company. Sometimes a Customer Advisory Board is managed out of a marketing department to nurture advocates and generate insights for case studies. In other organizations, these boards are run out of one of the post-sale functions such as Success Management or Customer Operations.

Regardless of who manages your company's Customer Advisory Board program, it is incredibly important for you, as a Chief Customer Officer or post-sale leader, to participate directly in the program and engage actively in the dialog. Your company is asking your customer executives to invest their time in sharing their insights and experience with you. Investing your time in return demonstrates that you are sincerely interested in hearing from them. Plus, participating is a great way to efficiently gather actionable input that can inform your decision-making and priorities. Resist the urge to delegate this responsibility to others.

Gemma Cipriani-Espineira was recently promoted to be the CCO of Chili Piper, a scheduling software solution for sales teams. Chili Piper launched a Customer Advisory Board and created five different Customer Advisory Board groups that correlate to their five target customer personas. While many companies operate the Customer Advisory Board out of a marketing organization, Gemma recommends that they be led by the CCO and his or her customer-facing teams.

She explained, "This direct interaction is a treasure trove. We do it every quarter with each group and I attend all of them. I hear directly from people who are our ideal customer profile. We get feedback on our Go-to-Market strategy and our product roadmap. It means something to them that the Chief Customer Officer is actively engaged in the conversation." These Customer Advisory Board sessions help Chili Piper's leadership team better understand the needs, trends, and experiences of their customers.

Understand Your Customer Needs

Not all Chief Customer Officers need to have deep product knowledge or industry expertise to be effective leaders. There may be certain types of companies where a specific background is required. However, I have found that the most important characteristics include curiosity and the sincere desire to learn about the needs and expectations of your customers. Sometimes, bringing fresh eyes to your customer experience can uncover useful new insights.

Deeply understanding the needs and expectations of your customers is important for three reasons. First, you will be a more compelling advocate for your customers with your various internal stakeholders. You can confidently offer first-hand insight that informs decision-making at different levels of your organization. Second, your knowledge provides context for prioritizing where to allocate your team's resources. You will develop a much better feel for how the work of your organization contributes to the outcomes expected by your customers. Third, your advocacy builds credibility with your customers directly by demonstrating that you are trying to listen to them and understand their needs. We all want to be heard and appreciate the effort it takes to truly listen.

Leveraging Insights From Your Customer Listening Posts

There are a number of great channels available that provide feedback about how your customers experience your products and services – customer surveys, in-product analytics, feedback sessions from your internal teams, call driver analysis, churn reason codes, and customer advisory boards.

Anita Toth recommends setting up a Voice of the Customer (VOC) program to help you keep track of all your customer feedback from across your various listening posts. A well-structured VOC program can provide an umbrella for all these activities and can help you feel more confident in the quality of the data you are collecting.

CAREER ACCELERATOR

Take a sincere and ongoing interest in learning from the data and feedback gathered across your VOC listening posts.

Here are a few ideas for turning this information into actionable insights so you can prioritize where you spend your time and resources.

Review Your Customer Survey Data and Discuss It With Your Leadership Team

There is a saying that "feedback is a gift." There is a good chance that your organization surveys your customers – after support cases, after implementations, after using your product or service, after an interaction with your employee, or as part of an ongoing NPS program. Take the time to review the results. I recognize this activity can be a slog and that you probably have plenty of other things to do. While the quantitative results are important and may provide trends for your KPI dashboard, the real gold is in the qualitative feedback. What are your customers saying in the few minutes they invested to provide you with their input?

Reviewing the qualitative feedback creates an opportunity for you to hear their input and translate it into insights for your organization. How do they feel about your product or service? How do they describe their interaction with the people at your company? What do they say about the experience that is provided through your various touch points?

Be on the lookout for trends that you can share with your executive peers, your product and marketing teams, and your sales leaders. Listen for the stories. If you are not representing the voice of your customers, it is unlikely that there is another group that offers that insight. Also, review these trends with your own leadership team so you can identify strengths to reinforce and opportunities to improve.

Walk in The Shoes of Your Customer

When I worked at RingCentral, I led a portion of new hire orientation for employees that recently joined the company. At the time, RingCentral sold internet-based phone solutions for small businesses. Together, I would take our new hires through the experience of buying, setting up, and using our products.

For example, we would visit the RingCentral website to review the marketing materials, call the sales center to hear how our sales teams describe the benefits, and place an order for a new phone system. A few days later, we would receive the phone hardware through the mail, open the box, and go through the experience of setting it up. We would get help from the implementation advisor, visit the self-service website, and call the support center. We discussed what worked well and what could be improved. You get the picture. This was a great way to experience firsthand what your customers go through. You can go through the same steps for almost any product or service you sell.

Watch Your Customers Experience Your Product or Service

Even if your product is not a physical product, you can still go through a similar process. Scott Cook, the co-founder of Intuit (the financial software company), introduced the customer research practice he called "Follow Me Home." This became a foundational methodology for Intuit's innovation process, and the process still lives on today. The principle is that by watching customers in their actual homes or businesses, you can observe how they use the product, and what they are doing at the time they face a challenge. This firsthand awareness can provide tremendous insight that you might not get by just asking them questions or having them fill out a survey. This type of experiential learning enables Intuit to make easy-to-use software, such as QuickBooks and TurboTax, that is used by tens of millions of customers and small businesses.

Ask Customers About Their Experiences

This approach seems quite simple but is often overlooked. As an organizational leader, many of the interactions you may have with customers can become quite transactional. Maybe you need to respond to an email request. Perhaps you are engaged in resolving an escalation. Maybe you meet customers at an event.

While addressing the situation at hand is important, always take opportunities to solicit feedback about their experience working with your team or your solution. When leaders genuinely ask other leaders for specific input, this interest creates an opportunity for mutual learning and frequently generates the type of valuable insight you hope for.

For example, you might ask, "What could we have done better," "What value did you get out of the discussion with the team member," or "What are the key differences between us and the solution you previously used?" Ask specific questions rather than just the throw-away phrase, "Let me know if you have any questions or feedback." Importantly, take note of the responses and use them to drive change in your business.

These examples are just a few of the ways that you can understand the needs of your customers. There is no shortage of additional touchpoints. You must show this interest consistently and with deep curiosity. If you choose not to manage this type of feedback process internally, you can also hire third-party vendors to help you gather feedback and generate insights for your business.

Be the Internal Champion for Your Customers Within Your Company

Your customers need an advocate who understands their needs, concerns, and frustrations. You can be that voice. Regardless of where you report or your scope of responsibilities, your customers count on your leadership to advocate for them within your company. You speak on their behalf due to your understanding of how they use your solution and how your service helps address their business challenges. Most companies do not take this approach. This advocacy can be a clear point of differentiation for you to have a customer-centric mindset.

CAREER ACCELERATOR

Be a vocal advocate internally for the needs, interests, and frustrations of your customers.

This task needn't be overwhelming. Here are a few simple actions you can take that can make an impact.

Share Priorities With Your Peers

For example, product teams gather input from customers from a variety of listening posts. Your organization is potentially interacting with customers all day, every day and inevitably gathers information about how your products and services can continue to meet their needs.

Effective leaders take this information and distill it into priorities that can be easily digested by their product teams. This is different from just giving your peer organizations a laundry list of requests. You can be most impactful by working with your team to identify the most important areas for development or improvement and then sharing the context of those expectations with your peers.

Tell the Stories of Your Customers in Public Settings

People remember stories. Take opportunities to tell stories of how your customers' lives got better because of your product or service. Volunteer to tell the stories at your company all-hands meeting. Write about these stories on a blog or LinkedIn. Create opportunities for your marketing team to hear about client stories for their case studies. Even better, invite your customers to your all-hands meetings and let them tell their stories in their own words.

An added benefit of telling stories publicly is that it allows your employees to make an important connection between the work they do and the outcomes that are delivered for customers. By speaking on behalf of your customers, you build your internal brand as an advocate for their interests.

Star Hofer is the CCO of PartnerStack, a leading partner management software platform. She takes opportunities at each company all-hands meeting to share customer stories with the broader organization.

"The stories allow the engineers to really see that the result of their hard work is actually being used," Hofer says. "Sales teams can use them in their prospecting, and Marketing can use them in case studies. Even HR can use them when talking to candidates." These types of customer stories create ways that relate the work across organizations to customer outcomes. The CCO can be a memorable vehicle for telling these stories.

Leverage Your Knowledge and Experience to Add Value to Your Clients

Tiffany Taylor leads the Success and Education organization for Handshake, a company that prides itself on being the number one way that college students get hired. This was her first role working in the private sector. Prior to joining Handshake, Tiffany had worked for more than thirteen years in the field of higher education.

Tiffany has already been promoted several times in less than four years at the company. One of the areas where she stands out is her ability to bring her past experience to bear when working with the college and university leaders that make up an important segment of Handshake's customers. She has a deep understanding of the inner workings of educational institutions at all levels, from professors to professionals and policies to pupils.

"What I have in spades is years of experience in higher education," she states. "I've written policy for higher education in California. My efforts have helped shift a very technology-focused company to build market share with our higher education partners. They are proud to be a Handshake partner. We are building this and changing this industry together."

Laurence Leong is the VP of Customer Success at Jamf, a publicly traded company that makes mobile device management software. One of the ways that his teams add value is to help clients understand how they are performing compared to others. He recommends using phrases like "other customers like you do X" or "your use of our solution looks like Y compared to other similar customers." As a leader with visibility to customers across your entire base, you have a point of view that is unique.

Leong states, "Your clients may have experiences with your product or service from maybe one, two, or three companies. The knowledge from your team comes from working with hundreds or thousands of customers."

Create Opportunities to Engage Other Departments in Customer Experience Design

Layton Chaney is a strategy consultant who works with many Customer Success organizations. A client was struggling to develop a culture that prioritized delivering great customer experiences.

They said, "I've come to the conclusion that you cannot have ultimate customer success without a powerful team that feels included in the conversations around the customer. If the CEO or CFO is just having them focus on initiatives to appease upper management or the board, it can be a challenge to execute."

To overcome this cultural barrier, Layton worked with the client to create a Customer Success committee that included representatives from different departments, stating that "They would come together and define strategies for what I would call 'wow moments.' They were looking for opportunities for the customer to experience something great."

The team identified and implemented a number of ideas to improve the experience including delivering free virtual training to help customers learn to use the product. They also created an offering that would bring team members from various departments to do onsite visits with certain high-value clients.

Layton described that "The value was that this program was building the internal passion around the customer across teams. It helps overcome a situation where most of your company may not even know what you do because it is all in a silo."

After a year, Layton and the client identified two important outcomes. First, the customer NPS scores and retention rates increased measurably. Second, there was internal excitement about how the various teams collaborated to improve client outcomes. This generated momentum within the company for what the teams could accomplish when working together: "When there is word of mouth within the company of what you can do to build a culture around your customers, the execution is just better."

CHAPTER REVIEW

QUESTIONS TO CONSIDER

- Which customers and customer segments are most important to the future growth of your business?
- How would you describe the quality of your relationships with your most important customers?
- What listening posts do you use to gather VOC and input from your customers?
- What are the common trends that you and your organization hear from those listing posts?
- How well do you understand how your products and services deliver against customer needs?
- What operating mechanisms are in place to prioritize and share insights with your stakeholders?

ACTION PLAN

- Identify three to five key customers to establish or enhance your relationship with over the next 60 days.
- Gather data from your various listening posts to identify at least five trends and five interesting insights.
- Discuss the trends and insights with your own leadership team to define any actions to take.
- Share key insights and prioritized recommendations with the appropriate functional stakeholders.

Strategy 4
Communicate Effectively and Tell Stories

I remember the first time I presented at our annual Sales Kickoff meeting when I worked at Marketo. I had an opportunity to share the business strategy and new offerings for the upcoming year related to our customer enablement and education services. I had rehearsed my presentation and felt ready to go. While I had spoken at my functional all-hands and all-company meetings, I had never been on a big stage in front of hundreds of team members and partners before. I was pretty anxious.

When my name was introduced, my heart started to race. I got up from my seat, walked to the side of the stage, and as I started to walk up the stairs, I stumbled, banging my knee. I barely caught myself with my hands before crashing on the steps. My colleagues held their collective breath as they waited to see if I was okay.

I got up and walked to the podium, where I made a joke saying, "My onboarding experience has just gone awry." The joke generated hearty laughs and put me at ease. I delivered my presentation and took questions. Even with the nervous stumble during my entrance, my opportunity to speak at the Sales Kickoff meeting helped me build confidence that I could successfully get in front of an increasingly large and influential audience.

As a CCO or aspiring CCO, you must develop your ability to communicate the vision, strategies, and results of your organization's work to an increasingly broad set of stakeholders. Your audience looks for signals from you to instill them with relevant information, direction, confidence, and the values of your customer-facing teams. These are skills that take practice to master and that become more natural over time.

In the early stages of your leadership journey, these audiences may just include your managers in your leadership team meetings or your entire team at your functional all-hands. Your communications may have a practical impact, enabling your teams to clearly understand the goals of the organization and information that is important for them to do their jobs.

As your career progresses, you may have opportunities to speak at your company's all-hands meetings or at small customer events. This provides an opportunity to highlight your strategy, mission, and priorities to audiences outside your team.

As you take on more executive roles in your company like Vice President or Chief Customer Officer, you may present to your CEO's staff, at company Board of Directors Meetings, or during a keynote at your annual customer conference. This gives you an even broader opportunity to demonstrate the value and impact of your customer-facing organization to your key stakeholders.

This chapter highlights a number of communication skills and behaviors that demonstrate your evolving progression as a customer-facing leader. This chapter also points out opportunities where you can hone your ability to get your message across.

Practicing the Art of Storytelling

Great performers have a voice. That voice is the result of years of practice in rehearsals, on stage, and in front of a mirror. Their voice reflects their personality and the expectations of their audience. Performers adjust their communication style to the setting. When they are on stage performing, they are playing to their fans. If they are being interviewed on a late-night show, their message is targeted at those watching the show.

CCOs and other post-sale leaders need to have a voice as well. Not just one that you hear, but a voice that is internalized by your stakeholders and that sets a tone for the customer-facing interactions of your company. Think of it as your CCO brand identity.

Star Hofer had been recently promoted to be Chief Customer Officer after two years at PartnerStack, a company that makes a software platform that supports affiliate, referral, and reseller channel partners. Her path to the role was ultimately accelerated by overcoming one of her fears and by leveraging one of her unique strengths – her ability to tell compelling stories.

Early on in her tenure at PartnerStack, she tended to steer clear of putting herself in positions that might make her uncomfortable or at risk of being seen in a negative way. So she generally avoided using her superpower storytelling ability.

"At a previous company, I was told to avoid the spotlight," she told me. "If you did this or this or this, you could get fired. I was used to having to button up everything so much that I had this insecurity of being let go."

Over time, Star made a decision that she no longer wanted to bury her superpower. "I had an a-ha moment. I am a storyteller. I can speak in front of my peers. I can speak in front of any audience. In all our all-hands meetings, I would talk about the numbers and then share a success story."

Here is her advice about storytelling: "It is very important to know the audience and read the room to understand the impact my words are having on somebody. If I am going to speak to an audience, I already know what I want the outcome to be. I will be very explicit in my mind."

Star had completely changed her approach and mindset. Her executive leaders noticed her ability to use storytelling to inform the company of her team's results and impact. She believes this ability was one of the reasons she was promoted to CCO. It was an effective way to ensure that the customer lens is always at the forefront of decisions across the broader PartnerStack organization.

CAREER ACCELERATOR

Practice to become an effective storyteller. People remember stories. Share stories publicly and frequently.

Remember those earlier chapters about building relationships with customer executives, gathering feedback from different Voice of Customer channels, and optimizing business results for your company? Those interactions and insights can be excellent sources of material for developing your stories.

Let's talk now about how you can leverage your communication skills and storytelling ability to drive better outcomes.

Define the Right Message for the Right Audience

As your career evolves, you may want to make a conscious effort to develop your communication skills and broaden your impact. You need to be able to deliver individualized, targeted messages that fill the needs of each different audience. You don't want to be too deep in the weeds when you share information with your CEO and executive staff. You also don't want to be too high-level when running your weekly staff meeting.

You should focus on five key audiences:

1. Your own organization that includes your managers, team members, and partners
2. Your customers and prospects
3. Your company's entire employee base, including key cross-functional teams
4. Your CEO and the executive staff
5. Your board of directors

Let's discuss the skills and behaviors required for each of these audiences.

1 - Your Organization and Direct Reports

Your leadership team and your employee base need to understand the strategies, priorities, and resources available for them to do their day-to-day customer-facing jobs. Those team members will want to know how they are performing against expectations, what they can be doing to improve, and what skills are necessary to grow in their roles. The time horizon most relevant for your current organization is the current month, quarter, or fiscal year.

As an organizational leader, you cannot do everything on your own. So you need to establish strategies, norms, and behaviors that help your team understand what is expected from them as they perform their jobs. What are the customer experiences they are expected to deliver? How do they interact with and execute handoffs with other organizations? What is their ability to go above and beyond for customers? When is it appropriate to escalate and ask for help? Will there be any consequences?

There are many great books and articles about effectively leading your organization. You can get a list of the ones I recommend at www.ccoplaybook.com/resources. All I will say here is that rising post-sale leaders can use your interactions with your direct reports and employee base to practice defining your messages and hone your voice. These interactions offer a regular, low-risk way to develop your customer-facing strategies, refine your priorities to improve, and communicate your vision for how your team delivers experiences to your customers. Be conscious of how you can make the most of your one-to-ones, staff meetings, town halls, and all-hands meetings to practice this important skill.

Short-Term Strategic Priorities and Initiatives

Leaders are counted on to define and communicate the improvement priorities their organizations must achieve to support the needs of the business into the future. For post-sale organizations, these initiatives can include the development of new processes, experiences, and handoffs to drive better outcomes for their customers. The priorities can also include initiatives that improve team productivity and operational efficiency.

The audience for communicating strategic priorities and initiatives is often broader than just your own team. This can provide a level of transparency that is particularly valued by your cross-functional peers and by your company's executive team. They will want to know how your organization is allocating its resources to contribute to future growth and also to understand the dependencies that you may have on other teams.

This level of detail can be appropriate to share in your own all-hands meetings, meetings run by your cross-functional peers like Sales and Marketing, and also at your company all-hands. By having repeated opportunities to share your organization's priorities and key initiatives, you will reinforce the value that your team provides and demonstrate how the improvement initiatives are aligned to support desired company outcomes. This communication also provides clarity for what other teams can expect from your part of the business.

Customer Journey and Desired Experiences

Your direct reports and their teams benefit from your ability to clearly communicate how your customer-facing experiences are intended to operate. Even in situations where there are gaps or improvement opportunities, a well-designed customer journey helps customers move smoothly through the various steps in their interactions with your company. This situation sets expectations for how cross-functional teams should engage with the customer and also how individual team members support those designed experiences.

You may learn that not all steps in your customer experience are actually well-designed or well-executed. This creates opportunities for you and your teams to prioritize and drive the appropriate improvement initiatives. These types of improvements may also be the result of situational changes in your business. You may be expanding to a new customer segment, so you need to design a process to support that group. You may have to achieve a certain financial target that requires you to tradeoff investment in one set of experiences for another. The takeaway here is that you are creating transparency to the expected customer experiences and also to the areas where you are prioritizing improvement opportunities.

2 - Customers and Prospect Communications

Your customers are also an important audience for you to consider when designing your engagement model. You will certainly have plenty of opportunities to interact with them on a one-to-one basis through customer meetings and escalation management opportunities. However, you can create a systematic communication strategy that you can choose to deploy to achieve a more impactful outcome for you and your business.

Direct Communications with Customers

At some companies, the Chief Customer Officer or other post -sale leaders are the main points of contact for communicating with existing customers. This can create a more personal connection between the customer and your company. This specific contact point may also demonstrate that there is a leader who is making themselves available to ensure that their customer experiences are positive.

Consider whether any of these scenarios are appropriate for you:

- Do new customers receive an email from you welcoming them as customers?
- Do feedback survey requests come from you to show customers the importance of their input?
- Are you leading or participating in Customer Advisory Board meetings?
- Are you actively reaching out to key customers to share information and priorities?

You can be deliberate about the opportunities you create for yourself to establish credibility and awareness with your customers. This gives them confidence that they have a strong advocate on the executive team that is representing their needs and interests.

Customer Conferences and Events

After you master your messaging internally, you may be called upon to represent your company to groups of customers at conferences, company events, or on webinars. In these situations, you may be one of the few company representatives that these audiences ever hear from directly. Take time to define what impression you want to leave and how you want your audience to feel after you speak to them. Each different audience is commonly looking to you for learning, best practices, and reassurance that the company it counts on for a critical outcome has strong leaders. Early in your career, take opportunities to present at breakout sessions or in smaller group settings. As you build your skills and confidence, take on larger audiences and more keynote types of opportunities.

CAREER ACCELERATOR

Create opportunities to represent your company by talking, presenting, or moderating at customer-facing events.

3 - Your Company's Employee Base and Key Cross-Functional Teams

I am frequently struck by how little understanding there is internally regarding the work done by a Chief Customer Officer's organization. Most people at your company are probably familiar with a support team and how it helps your customers resolve their service or product issues. However, there may be much more limited understanding regarding the offerings and experiences provided by your other post-sale teams. Could these other teams explain the work and outcomes expected from your success management team? Your implementation or services team? Your education department?

Organizational Roles, Responsibilities, and Success Metrics

Your post-sale organization may be one of the largest teams at your company in terms of the number of employees at your company. Ensure that your stakeholders, particularly those that influence the resource allocation and budgeting process, understand the roles of those team members and the value of this investment. Reviewing the roles of the various functional departments in your organization along with their success metrics can be surprisingly valuable.

One best practice I have seen is to periodically do an "internal roadshow," where you meet with leaders and managers of various departments to give them an overview of your organization's structure, goals and objectives, and key initiatives. This can be a great way to ensure that key stakeholders hear directly from you and can ask questions that may be on their minds. In a hybrid work environment where employees may work more in their own functional silos, these cross-functional interactions can be extremely valuable.

Updates on the Status of Key Customers

You should create the appropriate amount of transparency and visibility to the status of key customers. This could include the status of their onboarding projects, their support tickets, their account health, or other critical interactions. Some of these statuses may be visible through your CRM, your customer success platform, a professional services automation solution, or a project management tracker. In other situations, you or your team may need to provide a more customized summary of results. You can also communicate progress in a weekly email summary, a dashboard, or through a messaging platform like Slack or Microsoft Teams. Regardless of the channel or level of detail, you will want to provide an appropriate level of detail for you and your team to operate your business.

Evolving leaders should be able to provide reports and dashboards that offer visibility to operational results and the status of projects that are important for your stakeholders to follow. These could include metrics such as retention rate, operating margins, support case CSAT, and customer health status. Reports could also include the status of initiatives that are in place to improve those outcomes. This type of communication may happen in email, Slack updates, reporting systems, CRMs, staff meetings, and all-hands. This is a fundamental skill of a leader. Establish the pattern of communication that works best for you.

Communication of Results Compared to Forecast and Plan

A successful Chief Customer Officer will have a firm understanding of their team's business results and how they compare to the expectations set as part of your fiscal year planning process. You can do this through forecast review meetings, reporting dashboards, or other presentations that provide high-level overviews of performance versus plan. In addition to providing visibility to the results themselves, you should also be positioned to provide context as to why the results are occurring.

For example, if you are exceeding your forecasted renewal rates, you should ideally be able to explain what is behind those results so that you can apply that learning for the future and repeat it for other customers. If your support case volume is much higher than expected, you want to be able to communicate the root cause so you can determine if any action needs to be taken within your organization or in collaboration with other departments.

4 - CEO and Executive Staff Communications

There may be certain times of the year when you have an opportunity to present to your CEO's staff or during another similar type of executive leadership forum like a strategy planning offsite. This creates an opportunity for you to demonstrate your ability to communicate at the appropriate strategic level for that audience.

Connect the Dots to Show the Value of your Team's Work

Are you able to clearly demonstrate the link between the work your team does and financial outcomes? Do you understand the levers that drive your business results? Do you understand what dependencies your teams have on other cross-functional organizations?

These types of executive presentations or strategy sessions are great opportunities for you to develop and enhance your internal brand. The outcome of these experiences can be significant for your career development. You will want to be seen as a peer of others on the executive staff, regardless of whether or not you report directly to the CEO or have the same level of title. You will want to demonstrate that your strategic thinking and ability to execute are commensurate with the senior-level role that you play.

Take the time to think about the goals you want to set for yourself ahead of these sessions, and practice your communications so you can have the impact you intend. You can also leverage the customer stories, feedback from the VOC, and other client interactions to help you accomplish these goals and make the discussion memorable.

Speak Up, Share Results, and Advocate for Yourself

If you are a CCO or on a career path to be a CCO, there is a good chance that you are a "people pleaser." You may be the type of leader that is considered helpful and kind, so when there is an issue with a customer to be handled or a tough business problem to be solved, people come to you and you step up. You may be the type of person who has a need to make other people happy, like your customers or colleagues, often at the expense of your own needs and desires.

Being a "people pleaser" comes with many of these very positive attributes, and likely has contributed to getting you to where you are in your career. But this characteristic may also limit your ability to recognize other steps you should be taking. Maybe you don't take credit for your great results because you recognize that there are so many other people involved in achieving those outcomes. Maybe you don't speak up when there are opportunities to expand your scope because you are concerned about hurting other people's feelings. Maybe you don't advocate for yourself to ask for a promotion when it is warranted.

This can lead to your frustration because leaders in other functions feel more comfortable putting themselves on center stage without hesitation. Sales leaders commonly take credit for "crushing the sales target last quarter" even though there is a long list of functions that made that possible. Maybe they even take credit for hitting the expansion sales numbers (which you may feel are largely the result of your team's work with existing customers… extra ouch!). Product leaders talk about the awesome new features that were delivered for customers and that will blow the pants off the competition.

Perhaps you see these communications as boastful and arrogant or that your peers are not team players. That may not be the case. Perhaps they are just more comfortable speaking about their results. Or maybe that is just what people expect to hear from a Sales or Product leader.

You may be asking yourself what people expect to hear from a CCO or aspiring CCO. First, you should speak up for yourself and your organization to share results. Take credit for the great work you and your team have done that drive positive outcomes for the company. Second, be aware of when your peers are taking credit for the work done by your organization. Find ways to share stories about the role your team played or how your organization collaborated with other teams to achieve those results. Third, advocate for yourself when working with your CEO and their staff. Be confident about the important role that you play on the executive team.

CAREER ACCELERATOR

Take credit for your team's successes. Connect the dots between work done and outcomes delivered.

5 - Board of Directors Meetings

Board of directors meetings give you an opportunity to interact directly with investors and other executive-level leaders. Board members are not only seeking to understand your organizational strategy and results, but they are also evaluating the quality of your thinking, communication style, and leadership. You will need to adjust your communication style to the level and expectation of the Board. Take the time to get input from your manager or other peers that have presented to this group before. Practice, practice, practice.

Kellie Capote, the Chief Customer Officer at customer success software platform Gainsight, has become an expert at presenting to her Board of Directors and has received tremendous kudos for her communications. According to Capote, Gainsight's Board of Directors appreciates her data-driven narrative with clear business impact, the way she integrates relevant customer stories, and how she connects the goals to an action plan with success criteria.

Here is what Capote shares as her guiding principles for creating a Board of Directors slide deck:

1. The Board of Directors slide deck should generally be no more than ten slides.
2. Every slide title should tell the key takeaway/story. Don't use generic titles. Always include an Executive Summary.

3. Metrics should include leading and lagging metrics. High-value activities should drive these metrics. Draw the connections for the audience.

4. For any lowlights/learnings, include an action plan to mitigate them and how you will measure success.

5. For highlights, underscore how and why you were able to achieve these outcomes (e.g. what initiatives, intentional focus areas).

6. Include and be prepared to speak to customer stories for any callout in your presentation (churns, downsells, expansions).

7. Dig deep into the trends to help craft the narrative. You won't present all of this information, but some of this info may be included in the Appendix.

8. For the Key Initiatives/Action Plan slide, always include a red/yellow/green status and success criteria. Tie back to lowlights/ headwinds, etc. Show how the Strategic Initiatives tie to the overall company initiatives and goals.

9. Lead with data and connect it to customer stories and measurable actions in every slide.

10. Be confident and succinct with your presentation. What are the three takeaways for each slide that you want to share? Don't present every bullet in your deck.

11. Show ownership of your path forward and rallying cry to drive towards a stretch goal. Demonstrate the operational rigor you've put in place to get there.

12. Whenever you include a chart or table, include a key takeaways box to highlight the "so what."

To download Capote's slide deck template that you can use as a starting point for your own Board of Directors slides, visit www.ccoplaybook.com/resources.

CAREER ACCELERATOR

Practice your speaking points before presenting to your Board. Get advice from your CEO and CFO.

Sean Jacobsohn is an investor and corporate board member in his role as a partner at Norwest Venture Partners, a leading venture capital and growth equity investment firm. During board meetings, Jacobsohn appreciates when CCOs provide transparency to results and when they highlight challenges in the customer experience. He explains that this transparency helps the board understand the business risks more clearly and also gives them an opportunity to see how the various parts of the company come together to address challenges.

"I would like to understand how the CCO is forecasting logo retention and which customers are at risk," says Jacobsohn.

"We might be able to help with existing executive relationships and we can bring other resources to bear."

If you want to get promoted to increasingly more senior customer-facing roles, you must master your ability to communicate information to different stakeholders and in different settings. Ask for feedback and be aware of whether you are having the desired impact on your stakeholders.

In this chapter, we talked primarily about the audiences, the content, and the situations where your communications and storytelling can have the most impact. There are a number of great resources available to help you develop your presentation and speaking skills. You can download a list of recommended resources at www.ccoplaybook.com/resources.

CHAPTER REVIEW

QUESTIONS TO CONSIDER

- Who are the best communicators and storytellers at your company? What do they do that makes them so effective?
- How would you describe your ability to communicate effectively with your various stakeholders? What are your strengths? What are your growth opportunities?
- Which audiences are most important for you to communicate with over the next three to six months? What messages are most important to get across to them?

ACTION PLAN

- Set up meetings with one to two leaders at your company who are the most effective communicators and storytellers. Discuss with them your goals and what you might learn from them.
- Identify two new opportunities for you to present at an internal meeting to share your organization's goals, results, or progress against an important project over the next two to three months.
- Seek out an opportunity to present at an executive meeting (CEO staff, board meeting, or cross-functional staff meeting) about an initiative you are driving.
- Create two stories related to how a particular customer has benefitted from using your company's solution or how their relationship has grown with your company over time.

Strategy 5
Demonstrate Strategic Thinking

Chief Customer Officers are increasingly expected to be the visionary and strategic leaders for your customer-facing organizations. You need to demonstrate a strong commitment to delivering results for your current customers while also efficiently executing the strategic initiatives that will enable your team to support growth in the future. You will be expected to anticipate the variety of challenges that your teams will face and to have your organization prepared for when they get there.

"Everyone knows that sales and marketing are big levers," says Justin Sadrian, Managing Director at global private equity firm, Warburg Pincus. "I am getting excited about Customer Success as this is an area that CEOs and others don't talk about as much." Sadrian is currently on the board of five companies and previously served on the board of more than a dozen other companies. He has seen firsthand the value that strong CCOs can deliver to a fast-growing organization.

He goes on to say, "Defining the actual strategy is only half the battle. You need the implementation and follow through to drive the change."

In this chapter, you will learn about four techniques that demonstrate your strategic thinking and execution skills:

1. Create strategies for how your various teams can be aligned and work together.
2. Develop an annual, fiscal year plan to secure budget, resources, and commitment.
3. Respond strategically to changes in your business throughout the year.
4. Experiment, innovate, and learn quickly.

Get Your Post-Sale Team Leaders Aligned to Work Together

The CCO at one of my clients in the IT security space was facing a strategic challenge. The business was growing very quickly, but the company's CFO was challenging the CCO and his team to successfully support aggressive business growth without adding additional customer-facing team members. The company was hoping to improve operating margins and profitability to support its desired future valuation.

The CCO's leadership team identified a number of potential options, including introducing automation tools, expanding self-service resources, segmenting customers to reduce high-touch service to targeted groups of clients, and expanding the scope of certain roles to cover more customers.

My client pulled together the post-sale leadership team at a strategic planning offsite to work collaboratively through these options. They mapped out the desired customer experience through a journey-mapping exercise. They then analyzed the pros and cons of the various options.

The in-person collaboration enabled them to better appreciate the contributions that each functional team played. The CCO's team also recognized they could not move forward with all the options. They would need to make decisions and prioritize. They ultimately decided to focus their strategy on improving self-service resources and automation tools to make the work more streamlined for both their customers and the team members who supported them. That strategy became a primary theme in their annual planning process.

Chief Customer Officers need to be able to look across their entire business and coordinate the activities of their various departments to achieve their intended outcomes. At a strategic level, they often are expected to deliver great customer experiences in a way that encourages fast time-to-value, high retention rates, and aggressive product expansion. They also frequently need to do this in situations where resources are scarce and improving operating margins is a constraint.

You can achieve this delicate balance by following these four career accelerator tips:

Tip 1: Do Your Quarterly and Annual Strategic Planning as a Group

Involve your functional team leaders in the process to define the strategic initiatives and priorities across all of your groups. This will help them recognize the dependencies and tradeoffs that will need to be made across teams. Give them an opportunity to provide feedback and get a shared understanding of each other's plans. Highlight common strengths and challenges.

PITFALLS

Involve your management team early when defining your fiscal plan. Don't do it alone.

Tip 2: Create a Shared Incentive Structure

Create a shared incentive structure for your leadership team that depends on their ability to work together toward a common goal. Consider how to use your company's variable pay or incentive structure to get your leadership team invested in goals that span the entire post-sale organization. These often include your highest-level metrics such as retention rate, revenue expansion, or profitability targets.

Tip 3: Leverage Customer Journey Mapping

To give your functional leaders and team members visibility to what actually happens with customers as they experience your product or service, leverage customer journey mapping. Let the functional leaders visualize that customers do not operate in silos. Use a journey map to set expectations for how customers and employees should interact.

Tip 4: Design Efficient Handoffs Across Your Various Teams

Analyze your processes and look for opportunities to streamline handoffs as customers move between team members and across functional departments. For example, as your customers go from an implementation process to your support website or to your customer training portal, consider how information is shared across teams and how your touch points are designed to create a consistent experience. Simplify access to documentation that allows other team members to know what experiences preceded their touchpoints. Spend a few minutes reaching out to your colleagues to share important information.

In order to achieve this delicate balance, Chief Customer Officers need to ensure that their teams are coordinated, processes are automated whenever possible, and that duplication of work is minimized.

Develop a High-Impact Fiscal Year Plan and Budget

One of the most important decisions any leader makes is how to allocate budget and resources across his or her many potential teams, priorities, and initiatives. At the highest level, the board along with the CEO and CFO set the financial expectations for the company. They then ask the executive team to build a set of strategic plans to achieve those outcomes. The annual fiscal planning process takes place to evaluate alternatives and to negotiate investment decisions that demonstrate ways to operationalize the desired outcome.

Successful Chief Customer Officers develop strong strategic planning skills and leverage their position to secure the resources they need. They are most effective when they can measurably tie the work done by their team to the expected financial outcomes. They also recognize that their part of the business does not exist in isolation. The company often has a fixed amount of resources and investment to allocate across a tremendously wide number of potential priorities. It is a competitive market for acquiring budget and securing resources to invest.

CAREER ACCELERATOR

Make sure your fiscal year planning strategies, priorities, expected outcomes, and resources align with your company's plan.

Here are several skills to help you secure the resources you need:

Know Your Numbers

Effective leaders are familiar with the underlying metrics and levers that drive results. They understand how investments in one area impact other areas. I would encourage you to spend time with your finance partner to become fluent in the business model for your company overall and for each of the functional teams under your leadership.

Be Able to Show the Impact of Your Team's Work on Revenue and Profitability

Post-sale organizations are increasingly being asked to demonstrate the financial impact of the work they do. Several years ago, it might have been enough to intuitively understand that your organization needed to build out an onboarding process or that the company needed to hire people to get the renewal contracts signed.

At an executive level, arguing that the company "needs to hire additional people because your team is stretched thin or is too busy" is not particularly effective. When I worked at Gainsight, we could quantify that hiring an extra Success Manager would increase the overall retention rate by a certain percentage, increasing overall revenue by a predictable amount. See an example template at www.ccoplaybook.com/resources.

Volunteer to Lead a Cross-Functional Workstream in Your Company's Planning Process

While many of the steps in the fiscal planning process may require analysis within a company's functional silos like sales, marketing, or product, there are inevitably a number of high-level company strategies that require close collaboration across important functional leaders.

For example, depending on the business opportunity at a company, there might be a need to broadly improve the Go-to-Market process to accelerate revenue growth. Or perhaps there is a new product coming out the following year and there needs to be cross-functional work to ensure that the product has a successful launch. Consider finding ways to either lead these company-level strategic planning initiatives or to play an important contributing role.

Respond Strategically to Changes in Your Business

One of my recent clients found themselves in a situation where over the past few quarters, their sales organization generated a significant, un-forecasted increase in the number of new small commercial customers that purchased their supply chain business application software. The overall new sales bookings for the organization were right on plan. But there was a shift in the mix toward lower-end customers. The challenge was that smaller customers required almost as many resources to implement as larger ones. Each new customer took hundreds of hours of professional services time, regardless of the size of the ultimate revenue coming from the company.

This created a huge backlog to get customers configured and live. The influx of smaller customers also delayed the recognition of revenue to the company. Further, the backlog created potential dissatisfaction from customers whose launches were getting delayed. The client needed to redesign the implementation experience for this segment of customers, hire additional team members, and build out new self-service resources.

Rarely does anything go exactly as planned over the course of a year. Maybe there is an external shock that is out of your control such as a global pandemic, a supply chain disruption, or economic anxiety. Maybe there is a product release that flops. Or perhaps you bring in new clients that blow the sales forecasts out of the water. Whatever the situation, you want to have the strategic foresight to respond appropriately.

One of the benefits of being a customer-facing leader is that the list of potential scenarios is actually relatively limited, and the situations are also not likely unique to only your part of the business. To find solutions, you can look back on your previous experiences to help you anticipate what strategies you can employ. You can also reach out to peers who may have gone through similar situations.

Team members across your organization will be looking to you for direction. You should be able to anticipate the downstream consequences of certain foreseeable situations and confidently define your course of action. When you start to get a whiff of these trends in your business, you should consider taking the appropriate steps to keep things on track.

We cannot go through every scenario that you may experience. Let's review three examples of common situations that Chief Customer Officers and aspiring CCOs should be able to proactively anticipate and prepare for in their business.

1. Unanticipated increase in new customers that require onboarding or implementation
2. Pressure to scale without increasing headcount at the same pace as revenue growth
3. Changes in retention rate either up or down

Scenario 1: Significant Unanticipated Increase in the Number of New Customers That Require Onboarding or Implementation

If you see a significantly higher number of new clients than expected, you can expect that this situation has the potential to create a backlog of clients waiting to get assigned to your implementation team or onboarding process. Disappointed customers that thought they would get started quickly may start complaining about their experience to their salesperson and argue that they are paying for solutions that they are not able to use. Consider ways that you can prioritize your highest value customers, direct customers to self-service resources that may be a substitute for working with a live person, or leverage partner resources or other internal team members that can jump in to help with your new customer backlog.

Scenario 2: Pressure to Scale Without Increasing Headcount at the Same Pace as Revenue Growth

As companies grow revenue, there are commonly expectations that their operating margins will also improve. What this often means for the CCO and their organization is that they need to find ways to more efficiently support the growing customer base. Rather than necessarily adding additional people to support customers at the same pace as in the past, leaders need to find ways to streamline their work, improve their teams' productivity, and automate processes.

This very common challenge requires an executive to look for ways to improve productivity and efficiency. You, as a leader, need to be able to proactively think about the downstream impact of the decisions you need to make and consider how to make those tradeoffs. You may consider the impact on your customers, your team members, and your shareholders.

"CCOs need to be proactive rather than reactive to problems," explained Sean Jacobsohn, partner at Norwest Venture Partners. "They need to be proactive around building cross-functional relationships, understanding what customers are trying to accomplish, and getting ahead of potential problems."

One example is to add tools and resources that enable customers to do certain activities on their own without requiring them to interact directly with someone at your company. This could involve adding knowledge base articles to your support website, customer training on your education website, or webinars that enable many customers to learn best practice techniques at the same time.

A second example is to create segmentation that enables the delivery of differentiated experiences by customer value. Rather than investing a large number of resources for customers that might only be of low value to your company, you can provide different levels of service to different types of customers. Some of these customers may even be willing to pay premium fees for higher levels of service.

A third example could be to create a consulting partner delivery channel if you have an internal team that is doing its own onboarding and implementation for customers. This strategy often enables companies to better align the supply and demand of consulting resources with their desired business outcomes. This can happen through a subcontracting model, a co-delivery model, or by having your partners work directly with your customers.

Scenario 3: Significant Changes in Retention Rate That Drive Additional Focus on Churn

If you start to see your retention rate dip significantly, learning if there is an identifiable root cause is important. One way to gather this information is by having your team follow up with customers to get their feedback about why they chose to move away from your solution. You can ask them directly, interview them, or survey them.

Another way to gather this information is by having your team members track this information when they identify that a customer is going to churn. This type of "churn" or "loss" analysis can provide important quantitative and qualitative data that helps you determine the appropriate course of action to remedy. The data and insights can be presented in a way that provides visibility to metrics over time so you can compare results across different periods.

Experiment, Innovate, and Learn Quickly

I have run across an incredible number of high-potential, post-sale leaders that are talented, ambitious, and innovative. They want to achieve great outcomes for their companies and their customers. They also want to keep themselves on a forward-moving career path. They aspire to executive-level roles and are eager to learn from others and share their own best practices with their peers. Their future is very bright.

So, how do they drive innovation in their companies, while at the same time building up their knowledge of how to handle certain situations? One common theme I have identified is that they experiment quickly and learn from the results.

PITFALLS

Don't stick with something that clearly isn't working. Have courage to fail and learn quickly, then adjust.

Shannah Van Winkle is the Chief Customer Officer at Matillion, a software company that provides a data integration platform for fast-growing global businesses. She described that "one of the most important career accelerators for me has been a willingness to try out new strategies and processes to deliver better results for clients."

"In one of my past roles," she continued, "we worked with big companies like Cisco, PayPay, eBay, and American Express. Our Account Executives didn't have time to take care of them. We had no idea whether we were delivering value to them with our solution."

"I came in to see if we could build out an effective engagement process for these customers. First, we tried billing for it. Then we tried giving it away for free out of our services team. Then we moved it over to be part of the solution consulting arm. Finally, we developed it as part of a standalone customer success team that we sold as part of the enterprise license agreement contract."

Van Winkle said that she appreciated the opportunity to innovate and build different versions of a Customer Success process to find the one that was appropriate for that particular segment of customers. "There is power in being able to experiment and learn by doing," she said.

CHAPTER REVIEW

QUESTIONS TO CONSIDER

- What are the most important company-wide strategic initiatives over the next six to twelve months? What is your team's role in making progress against those initiatives?
- What competitive, industry, or customer trends are currently impacting your company in either a positive or negative way? How could your organization help respond to these trends?
- What new processes, tools, and experiences will you need to have in place to support the strategic needs of your business six to twelve months from now?
- Do you have the right organizational structure and leadership team that will be required to support your business six to twelve months from now? What changes might you need to make?

ACTION PLAN

- Identify two to three company-wide initiatives and define how your organization supports those goals.
- Define the three to four highest-priority improvements you need to have in place to deliver what your company will need from your organization six to twelve months from now.
- Set up a best-practice sharing session with a peer from another company that has tackled similar strategic initiatives or challenges. Understand what they learned.
- Identify one of these initiatives or improvements that you can make progress on over the next 60-90 days. Define the actions you can take to get started.

Strategy 6
Drive Change During Growth and Scaling

Todd Watts had just started as the Chief Customer Officer of Planview, a leading portfolio management and work management software provider that had recently grown through the acquisition of several competitors. Watts had been an executive at one of the acquired businesses. He was now responsible for integrating the resources, services, and cultures of the post-sale organizations across teams from three different companies. He recognized the importance of translating the company vision and high-level initiatives into what it meant for his customer-facing groups.

"What do each of our teams need to do to deliver more value to customers, to drive more renewals, to improve customer care?" he asked.

In situations when companies are integrating acquisitions, Watts recommends that Chief Customer Officers get familiar with the expected metrics and financial models so they can define the organization's priorities appropriately.

"It gives you a seat at the table when you can understand your investments and where the organization needs to place its bets," he explained. After building out the key performance indicators and defining the future-state customer experience, Watts then started to put in place initiatives to drive the required changes in business outcomes.

First, he focused on building a partner ecosystem to support the implementation of Planview software for new clients. This would improve customer time-to-value while also helping to improve profit margins. Second, he expanded the team's accountability to include the renewal process. He believed this would increase his team's engagement with the sales organization and lead to the retention of more customers. Third, Watts worked with his front-line team leaders to drive deeper understanding and more empathy for customers among their own teams.

He said that "You have to show passion for the customer that demonstrates you really want them to have the best possible experience. That mindset has to be deeply ingrained in what you do."

Integrating teams after acquisitions is one of many challenging situations that confront Chief Customer Officers and other post-sale leaders at growing companies. CCOs need to adapt their leadership skills, adjust to the new environment, and demonstrate foresight to prevent future roadblocks.

In this chapter, we will discuss a framework I created to help post-sale executives manage and scale their organization through periods of fast growth at their company. In the next chapter, we will then look at how to optimize your team performance during times of slow growth or contraction.

Scaling Your Organization with the Post-Sale SCALING™ Framework

Post-Sale leaders at fast-growing companies run into a fairly predictable set of challenges. They continuously need to evolve their organizations, systems, and processes to keep up with revenue growth. They contend with a difficult balancing act of delivering results to meet current period expectations while simultaneously executing against the strategic improvements they will need to have in place when the business is bigger.

CAREER ACCELERATOR

Balance your day-to-day priorities with the need to define and execute longer term strategic improvements.

Based on my work with dozens of clients and hundreds of post-sale leaders, I developed the Post-Sale SCALING™ Framework to help executives navigate their way through this growth journey. The Post-Sale SCALING™ Framework is a model that enables you to identify and analyze the strategic inputs that determine a post-sale organization's ability to support accelerated business growth. The seven different elements of the framework spell out the word S-C-A-L-I-N-G to make the framework easy to remember. The framework is intended to be used to determine improvement opportunities and to help leaders prioritize the appropriate strategic initiatives.

When I work with my clients, we review a series of discovery questions to help them diagnose their strengths, opportunities, and readiness for scaling in each of these seven areas. Then we prioritize those inputs that are most critical for the company to scale. Templates and resources related to the Post-Sale SCALING™ Framework can be found at www.ccoplaybook.com/resources.

Here are the seven strategic inputs to consider when scaling your organization.

Structure

Structure refers to how the people and teams are organized to work together. As you learned in an earlier chapter, post-sale teams can be organized by functions including Professional Services, Customer Success Management, Support, Education, Customer Operations, and Account Management. Another example is that as business needs evolve, organizations often have to decide whether to create specialization in areas that may orient around custom-

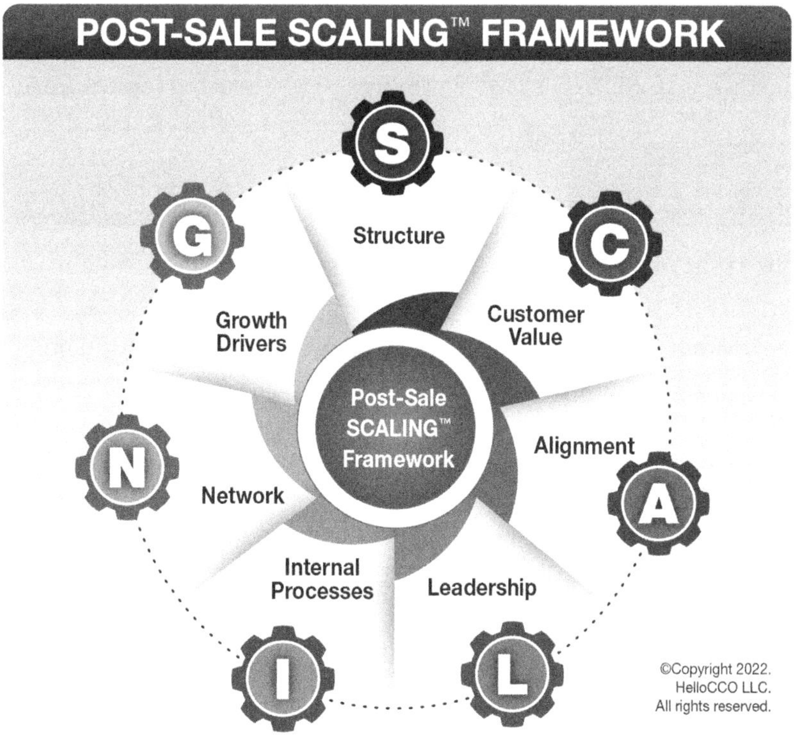

S TRUCTURE
How people are organized to work together

C USTOMER VALUE The experiences and outcomes customers expect from your organization

A LIGNMENT How your organization is aligned to your company, customer, and cross-functional objectives

L EADERSHIP The capabilities, values, and development of people who work for your organization

I NTERNAL PROCESSES The systems, data, processes and workflows that team members use to get their jobs done

N ETWORK The community of partners, vendors and thought leaders that create leverage and help erect competitive barriers

G ROWTH DRIVERS The ways that your post-sale team contributes to your company's growth and profitability

er size (i.e. SMB, Mid-Market, Enterprise), geography (i.e. US, EMEA, APAC), vertical segments (i.e. Retail, Health Care, Technology), or product line.

Examples of discussion questions to ask when considering the right org structure:

1. What functional teams are needed to support your business?
2. What customer segments could benefit from differentiated experiences?
3. What type of specialized roles or expertise is required?
4. How do various functions coordinate activities?
5. Can the current leaders and team members do the jobs required?

Examples of decisions to make:

- When to create a specialized implementation team to work with your new customers?
- When to design different offerings for customers based on their size or segment?
- When to organize teams by product, functional area, or geography?

Customer Value

Customer Value refers to the experiences and outcomes that your clients expect from your organization. For example, at different periods in your company lifecycle, clients may want faster time to value, prescriptive learning paths, or premium technical support services. Some clients may want additional self-service options. Others may want professional service offerings that provide higher touch experiences.

Examples of discussion questions to ask related to customer value:

1. What experiences do your customers need from each of your teams?
2. What value do your customers expect to receive from each function?
3. How will customers measure results now and in the future?
4. How can your post-sale experiences become competitive differentiators?

Examples of decisions to make:

- Whether to create packaged implementation offerings for new clients?
- How to design your success management cadence through your customer journey?

- Should you introduce fee-based premium support services?
- What self-service and in-person training solutions should you provide?

Alignment

Alignment refers to the position that your post-sale organization plays on the broader company team. What are the customer-facing and financial outcomes expected from your post-sale organizations? How do those targets change over time?

Early in your company's evolution, post-sale teams may focus on getting clients live, expanding adoption, or resolving support cases at all costs. Later as a company grows, there may be an increased focus on improving productivity metrics, increasing retention rates, or creating more predictable outcomes. Other companies may start to focus on ROI and profitability metrics.

Examples of discussion questions related to how you are aligned with company goals:

1. What role does your function play on the corporate team?
2. What outcomes does your company need from your organization?

3. How do your priorities align with company goals?
4. How will expectations for your organization need to evolve to support growth?
5. What incentives are in place to drive results?

Examples of decisions to make:

- What should be the KPIs and success metrics for your organization?
- How should you and your leadership team participate in the fiscal year planning process?
- What is the compensation structure for your teams?
- What outcomes are your organization uniquely expected to drive?
- What outcomes are your organization expected to contribute to for other teams?

Leadership

Leadership refers to the capabilities, values, and professional development of the executives and managers in your post-sale functions. It reflects the ongoing ability of these leaders to achieve the best results from the team members across your organization. Leadership also refers to your ability to recruit, retain, and develop the talent you will need now and in the future.

Examples of discussion questions to ask related to leadership development include:

1. Do you have the right leadership and management in place to scale?
2. Do they have the appropriate scope of responsibilities?
3. What new leadership or management roles will be needed in the future?
4. Do you have the pipeline of future leaders to support your growth?
5. How can you attract strong leaders that want to be a part of your growth plans?

Examples of decisions to make:

- Should you hire from the outside or promote/move someone internally?
- How can you accelerate the development of your leadership bench?
- Should you move an individual contributor into his or her first management role? When?

Internal Processes

Internal Processes refer to the systems, processes, and data that your team uses to support its activities and decision-making. Your teams probably use dozens of technology solutions today. Are they improving your team's productivity? Are those the same systems and tools you will need in the future? Do you have the right workflows and handoffs in place to deliver the desired customer experiences to your target customers? Do you have the data, reports, and dashboards you need to inform the growing number of decisions your teams need to make?

Examples of discussion questions to ask related to internal processes:

1. What systems, processes, and tools are needed to deliver desired results?
2. What resources are required to improve productivity?
3. Are you optimizing, simplifying, and automating workflows to enable scale?
4. How do you track the KPIs and metrics to identify insights and inform decisions?

Examples of decisions to make:

- What tools should you invest in for your teams?
- How to design the internal handoffs across your cross-functional partners like sales?
- When to initiate and how to grow a post-sale operations team?
- What automation is required to improve customer experience and streamline internal workflows?

Network

Network refers to the community of partners, vendors, and thought leaders that create leverage for your company. This network also enables you to erect competitive barriers around your solutions and creates differentiation.

Companies with people-intensive onboarding processes may need to create a network of consulting delivery partners to support more complex implementations. Companies in new product categories often want to build relationships with thought leaders to help generate interest in the new solutions and to share best practices with early adopters.

Examples of discussion questions to ask:

1. Do you have a partner ecosystem of people, services, and systems?
2. Are you building a network of product advocates and thought leaders?
3. How do your partners and advocates help you erect barriers to competition?
4. Could partners augment your internal delivery capacity or improve your financials?
5. How could partners help achieve better customer experiences and outcomes?

Examples of decisions to make related to your network:

- When should you build a consulting partner delivery ecosystem?
- When should you establish a customer or partner community?
- When should you create a Customer Advisory Board?
- What thought leaders should you partner with for your customers and prospects?

Growth Drivers

Growth Drivers refer to the ways your teams directly contribute to revenue growth and profitability. If you work in a consumption-based business, getting your customers using your product quickly and broadly might be a goal. For other types of fast-growing companies, your post-sale teams may be directly accountable for driving renewal contracts, expanding existing relationships, or delivering professional services revenue and margins.

Examples of discussion questions to ask:

1. What financial results are expected from your organization?
2. How do you quantify and measure the impact of your team's work?

3. How does your team contribute to retention and revenue growth?
4. What revenue, cost management, and profitability outcomes are expected?
5. What are the unit economics of your cost-to-deliver for your customers?

Examples of decisions to make:

- Whether or not to take accountability for sales quota including renewals or expansions?
- When to invest in self-service resources to improve productivity and financial metrics?
- When to automate workflows and processes to limit the need for high-touch experiences?
- What changes should you make to improve your cost-to-deliver?

There are more resources available related to the Post-Sale SCALING™ Model at www.ccoplaybook.com/resources.

These materials offer you a simple way to ensure that you are considering the full range of strategic alternatives as your business grows.

CHAPTER REVIEW

QUESTIONS TO CONSIDER

- Which of the seven strategic inputs defined in the Post-Sale SCALING™ Framework are strengths of your organization? Which are opportunities for improvement?
- Which of the seven strategic inputs are most important for your company to be able to sustain or accelerate its business growth over the next twelve months?
- What are the two to three highest priority improvement initiatives you need to get in place to be able to support your company's growth over the next year?
- What changes to people, processes, and systems are required to support your team's ability to execute against these two to three improvement initiatives?

ACTION PLAN

- Assess your team's strengths and opportunities using the Post-Sale SCALING™ Framework.
- Identify two strategic inputs that need to be improved to support your company's growth.
- Propose two to three changes or improvements that need to be executed to achieve those goals.
- Get alignment with your manager or executive team on prioritization and any resources required.
- Engage with your leadership to ensure you are appropriately balancing your focus on short-term results and any longer-term improvements to support the future needs of the business.

Strategy 7
Maximize Opportunities During Economic Uncertainty

During the Great Recession of 2007-2009, US Gross Domestic Product (GDP) declined significantly while unemployment briefly reached 10%. It was the worst economic downturn since the Great Depression in the 1930s. Industry leaders often use economic downturns to double down on R&D spending, invest in hiring talent to meet future needs, and acquire businesses that have great teams and products but that may be struggling financially. Apple, Facebook, and Google followed this pattern.

However, many more companies struggled significantly during those same years. Many public companies' stock share prices dropped, leading to decreases in the valuation of privately held companies as well. Employees worried about getting laid off, limiting their willingness to take risks that could drive innovation but that could also expose them to failures that made their jobs more vulnerable. Customers cut back on spending, driving down demand for products and services. This led to a massive contraction in the economy which included technology, retail, financial services, and many other sectors.

Leading Your Business Through Periods of Flat Growth or Contraction

So what is a Chief Customer Officer expected to do in this situation? For many of us, navigating the reality of the new post-pandemic, hybrid work-life is difficult enough. Now, add the uncertainty of the economic business cycle headwinds. This combination could put even the most experienced leader on edge. As I write this book, inflation is high, interest rates have jumped, and the stock market has dropped significantly. Anxiety about the future abounds and a recession may be happening or is just around the corner. The immediate economic future is uncertain.

Focus on Keeping and Growing Your Existing Customers

During difficult economic times, holding onto their existing customers is even more important for companies. Therefore, the role of the Chief Customer Officer becomes increasingly indispensable. As your company's sales pipeline slows and it takes longer to bring in new customers, you can become an internal champion for the need to maintain and grow revenue from your existing customer base. This should be your sweet spot. If you haven't received attention from your executive team in the past, you are likely to be in the spotlight whether you like it or not. You might as well embrace the visibility.

Your teams are closest to your customers and can quickly identify changing trends in their sentiment and behavior. You maintain personal relationships with key-client executives and can leverage those interactions to learn about the decisions being made at those companies. Importantly, you likely manage one or more of the functional teams that contribute to the key levers of customer retention, operational efficiency, and organic growth.

"Customer retention is critical in any business but even more important now because your customers are slashing their budgets," says Sean Jacobsohn, partner at Norwest Venture Partners and board member at several leading SaaS companies. "You have to protect your product by reminding your customers of the ROI they are getting."

The most important thing you can do when you start to experience an economic downturn is to begin your contingency planning and listen closely to what is happening with your customers and prospects. Don't wait. Be proactive. Christine Rimer, CCO of retirement plan software platform, Guideline, recalled the catchphrase from the television drama Game of Thrones that "Winter is Coming." CEOs and CFOs tend to follow certain predictable patterns during business downturns. You should be prepared to rationalize your budgets, prioritize your spending, and drive efficiencies in your business operations.

During economic downturns, smaller companies may need to focus on conserving cash because their prospects for additional fundraising may be more limited. Larger companies may need to find ways to preserve their profit margins, which puts pressure on teams to decrease costs to match potentially lower revenue.

The Post-Sale SCALING™ Framework introduced in the last chapter still provides a useful approach for assessing the situation and determining your strategy to move forward. There are five elements of that methodology that will be particularly useful for you to focus on.

Alignment - Clarify Expectations with Your CEO and CFO

During times of business weakness and uncertainty, you must have clear alignment with your executive team about the role that your organization is expected to play on the corporate team and the results that your team is expected to deliver. Your CEO, CFO, and Board of Directors are likely to be intensely focused on finding ways to optimize revenue and profitability.

You may want to consider applying that same lens to your own decisions and actions. Even if you are not involved in all the decision-making around staffing levels, cost management, and investment prioritization, you should assume that scrutiny will ultimately come around to your organization. If you get informed about decisions that could impact your team late in the process, don't get defensive. Just be ready! In either case, ask your CEO and CFO directly what they need from you and your team.

You should expect that your organization will be counted on to find ways to maintain (and even grow) retention rates. You can also anticipate that any requests to increase headcount in your organization to reflect these higher expectations for gross retention rates and net retention rates may be met with blank stares. Your CFO will be looking for you to find ways to improve operational efficiency and "do more with less." So, you should expect that you will need to think strategically about how you allocate your resources and prioritize your improvement initiatives to meet your targets.

PITFALLS

Be ready to adapt to new priorities from your CEO and CFO during challenging business cycles.

Customer Value - Reallocate Resources to Optimize ROI and Impact

In this type of challenging business situation, your company will become more dependent on revenue and growth coming from your existing customer base. This means that as an organization, you will want to focus your efforts to ensure that your customers are getting the value they expect from your products and services. You will be managing your business to maximize retention rates and to increase opportunities for revenue expansion.

Given this urgency, you may feel the need to ask for even more resources to ensure that you can achieve those goals. However, you can anticipate that you will get pushback from your CFO and CEO. What is more likely is that your organization will be slightly more immune to cutbacks that often face sales and marketing teams in these types of scenarios.

Even in this situation, you have various strategic options. As a CCO, you very likely manage multiple departments. This is potentially a great time to revisit your resource allocation across all your groups. Rather than thinking about your teams in silos, think about your organization as a whole.

If you have 100 employees spread across four functional teams, are there ways that you could re-allocate a few team members to help address any required changes to your strategy? Your executive team may not let you hire additional team members into the company, but there may be less restrictions around how you might move people around within your team of 100.

For example, if you need to create additional, self-service training courses so you can take the workload off your Customer Success Management team, perhaps you could shift a Customer Success Manager into that content development role for a period of time. If you require fewer implementation consultants because you have a drop in new clients, consider moving one of them to become an Enterprise Account Manager to provide more focus to your higher-value clients. These are just examples. The point is that you, as the Chief Customer Officer, have the responsibility for optimizing resource allocation across your whole organization, not just within each functional team. Too many leaders fail to make that distinction, so they miss opportunities to move people around to where their marginal impact is needed most.

METRICS THAT MATTER

You can reallocate resources across all your functional teams to maximize ROI, not just shift people around within functions.

Customer Value - Provide Best Practice Offerings and Experiences

Your executive team may also want to see improvements to your operational efficiency and productivity metrics. One of the most impactful ways to improve these metrics is for your teams to recommend best-practice solutions for your customers and move away from providing customized experiences for each client. Most customers do not want to be presented with an unlimited number of options for how to use your product or service. They frequently do not want to be asked to design a customized solution from a white sheet of paper. You and your team are the experts. Your customers look to you to recommend what they should be doing and to leverage what has worked for similar types of customers.

During difficult economic times or periods of slow business growth, leading with this type of prescriptive, best-practice-oriented approach has several benefits. First, this process is likely to work for a high percentage of your customers. They appreciate getting started using your product or service quickly by relying on what works for other similar customers. Second, prescribing best practices enables you to potentially leverage more junior team members because these resources can be trained on a limited set of product capabilities. Third, this strategy creates consistency in an experience that translates into more concise self-service training, a narrower range of potential use cases, and easier-to-resolve support cases. These all can translate into lower costs to serve a customer. A key watch-out is to be able to quickly identify those customers where this best-practice approach is not appropriate and enable them to customize their solution as necessary.

Growth Drivers - Be Able to Tie Investments to Revenue or Profitability Improvements

In times of slow or negative growth, you will likely find yourself negotiating for resources against your peer executives. Your CEO and CFO will be evaluating requests from many of those leaders who also want to preserve their teams, maintain their spending levels, or invest in certain initiatives they feel are critical to have in place when the business turns around.

Your spending and resource requests are likely to be considered in this broader context. Your executives will need to decide which initiatives are a higher priority than others. In these situations, you will want to be able to demonstrate the ROI of your investments as clearly as possible. That means you should try to connect the dots between the work your team does and its impact on your company's revenue or profitability.

One of my clients, Automox, recently made a significant investment in developing their self-service resources and educational content in an effort to reduce the need for high-touch support for certain segments of their customers. Under the direction of SVP of Customer Experience, Guy Lever, their Education leader, Sara Anderson, designed the training content, the learning management system, and the customer learning paths that enabled their clients to bypass many of the in-person interactions that had previously been required to complete their implementation. Within several months, customers were regularly using this new educational content. Their results showed that Automox was seeing a 75% reduction in the time it took to onboard a new customer, enabling the company to generate revenue faster and accelerate opportunities for customers to grow their adoption beyond the initial use cases.

Executing improvements in self-service resources is just one example of a way to help you accelerate time-to-value for your customers, decrease the number of support cases your team needs to take, and redirect customers that would otherwise feel like they need to talk directly to a live person. Do your best to tie your resource investments to measurable outcomes so you can demonstrate the results you are delivering from the improvement initiatives you invest in.

Growth Drivers - Leverage Implementation Partners

Implementation and professional services teams are notoriously low margin for many technology companies. You may not yet have created fee-based implementation offerings. Your existing offerings may not be attached consistently to contracts for your new customers. They also may be highly discounted if they are attached at all. Plus, optimizing resource management for these types of teams can be challenging under the best of conditions.

Particularly in times when demand for your professional service offerings may be low or hard to forecast, engaging with consulting delivery partners to supplement your team can be prudent. These types of partners are most commonly consulting organizations that work with your customers to help them design, configure, and implement your technology solution.

METRICS THAT MATTER

You can contribute to higher profits and valuation by optimizing Professional Services and implementation margins.

This type of relationship can be set up in different ways. One approach is where your customers contract directly with your partners. A second method is where these partners operate as subcontractors for your business. A third is a hybrid approach where you jointly deliver work for your clients. In any case, this type of delivery partner relationship helps you decrease the need for you to hire staff to meet your peak potential demand, and it enables you to leverage another company's resources to support your customers without adding headcount. If customer experience and outcomes are positive, working with consulting delivery partners can significantly improve your company's bottom line.

CHAPTER REVIEW

QUESTIONS TO CONSIDER

- How would you describe the current situation at your company?
- What challenges does your company face over the next year to turn around the business?
- How could your team assist in this turnaround?
- What results are expected from your teams now? How are they performing against those outcomes?
- What changes, if any, should you consider at this point given your company's situation?

ACTION PLAN

- Get alignment with your executive team and CFO on the current situation and what the expectations are for your team over the next six to twelve months.
- Define the two to three most important initiatives or actions you can be taking to ensure that you are on track to achieve those goals.
- Start an operating mechanism to create visibility and review progress against those high-priority initiatives or actions. Keep your executive team informed as well.
- Discuss status regularly with your CFO or Finance Business Partner. Seek input on how your team is performing against expectations and what more your team can be doing.

Strategy 8
Create and Share Thought Leadership

By 2013, Marketo was the leader in the growing category of Marketing Automation software that powered demand-generation marketing departments at companies around the world. One factor that made Marketo unique was its approach to being a thought leader as it created a new category of software. This approach would become a model for many other future software companies and the company's co-founder, Jon Miller, became an inspirational hero to an entire generation of digital marketers.

What was so different about Marketo's appeal? Instead of just teaching people how to use Marketo software, the company's model was to teach people how to be innovative digital marketers. They could certainly choose to use Marketo's software, but more importantly, the company wanted to help people become better marketers for their own organizations.

At that time, I was leading the Customer Enablement and Education organization at Marketo. We applied this mindset when working with our new and existing clients. We wanted to help them excel at their jobs, providing not just training on how to use the software but also providing best practices on how to drive marketing impact within their companies. For example, we designed an onboarding process that trained customers not just on the software features but also the basic marketing concepts underlying them like lead scoring, nurturing, and content marketing. Empowered by this corporate strategy to help marketers learn to do their jobs better, Marketo's community of users enabled the company to break away from competitors and create an extremely loyal customer base.

You too can be a thought leader. In fact, it is often a fundamental expectation of Chief Customer Officers and aspiring post-sale leaders that they provide expertise and value directly to their customers. Thought leadership can be demonstrated in any number of ways – writing, speaking, one-on-one discussions, publishing, etc. The point is that over the course of your career, you are developing and demonstrating skills as an expert in something … anything. You can then create opportunities to share that knowledge with customers, employees, executives, and peers.

What is Thought Leadership?

Thought leadership is the ability for you to share your expertise, stories, and struggles with a variety of different constituents in a way that can be leveraged by others. These audiences could include your customers and prospects, your executive team, your employees, your peers, and maybe even people who follow you on one or more of the common business-oriented social media platforms like LinkedIn or Twitter.

An important distinction between thought leadership and just talking is that your audience learns something. What you share creates a teaching moment. Maybe you are offering a new framework for solving a problem. Perhaps you are challenging the status quo. Or maybe you are sharing something personal that reveals a lesson for the audience.

Thought leadership does not need to be prize-winning or groundbreaking to be useful. It might even represent an embarrassing mistake or an example of a decision that goes horribly wrong.

You can communicate your thought leadership in a variety of forms. Some people like to write about their ideas in blog posts, LinkedIn updates, or the content marketing that your company publishes. Other people enjoy public speaking and create opportunities for themselves to share their ideas at company events, customer conferences, or industry conferences. Maybe you like to influence teams behind the scenes. You can share your experiences at your staff meetings, on calls with customers, or in internal training. Wherever you are in your career, have confidence that you can offer valuable insight to share. Find ways to get it out there.

Feel Confident That You Can Be a Thought Leader

You are likely already a thought leader. But do you think of yourself as a thought leader? If you are a manager of a team, you probably know more about certain functions of your business than your team members. As a customer-facing leader, you probably know more about your customer experiences and how your customers use your products or solutions than most people at your company.

Plus, you likely have a few areas of expertise that tie together different roles throughout your career. Maybe you have worked for several companies in the financial services industry. Perhaps you have worked for multiple start-ups. Maybe have experience working at publicly traded companies. Or maybe you have had several roles in a support organization or have had sales responsibilities. Establish a mindset that what you have experienced might be useful for certain groups of others to learn. Begin to create opportunities to share that knowledge. Identifying those wins that you have under your belt adds credibility to your stories and posts.

When I worked at Intuit, I learned an important lesson about creating thought leadership from Steve Bennett who was the CEO at the time. He introduced us to the concept of a Teachable Point of View (TPOV). A Teachable Point of View is a leader's way of laying the foundation for developing others. The concept was created by Professor Noel Tichy and focuses on helping leaders develop their points of view.

By encouraging us to create and share a Teachable Point of View, Intuit's CEO, Steve Bennett, took the pressure off that what we were intending to share needed to be brilliant and mind-blowing. Instead, we were encouraged to simply collect our thoughts and share them with relevant team members.

I remember that my first TPOV related to the importance of designing a great end-to-end experience for our QuickBooks Payroll customers. I used the analogy of a cruise ship where the passenger experience was thoughtfully designed – from getting luggage onto the ship, to getting people fed, to coordinating excursions, to disembarking at the end. I remember expressing the idea that you could apply these same experience design principles to our recurring revenue Payroll business. At the time, I was just sharing some simple observations with my team members and colleagues. Maybe it would resonate with them, and perhaps they would learn something. Either way, that was thought leadership. You can do this too! Here are a few easy ways to start.

Gather and Share Best Practices About How Customers Use Your Product

For post-sale leaders, this is an easy way to get started creating thought leadership. Take opportunities to talk to your team members to gather details about the characteristics of successful customers. Or reach out to customers directly and ask them. Find out what they do that enables them to benefit from your solution. How do they learn about your product or service? Listen for stories that you can retell. People love hearing stories, and stories make the information easier to remember. Then share these examples with your team and your colleagues.

Share Details of Processes That Generate Positive Outcomes for Clients or Internal Teams

Thought leadership can often come in the form of sharing processes that drive certain results. Maybe you get lucky, and the results are in fact awesome. But sometimes, even sharing details about how you designed an experience that didn't achieve the outcomes you wanted can be very insightful too.

One example could be how you segmented your implementation team and designed processes for them to follow so that they were able to consistently help your customers achieve fast time to value. Maybe your peers can learn from how you collaborated with your IT department to implement your new Learning Management Solution for your customer training website. That could be relevant for any department trying to implement new software. Or perhaps you can share how you created new support offerings with the help of your marketing and sales operations teams so they could easily be added to orders in your CRM system. This creates an opportunity to teach others how to work cross-functionally.

Speak at Customer Events or Your Company's Customer Conference

As you build your confidence, you may then feel ready to share your learnings with external audiences in more formal settings. Your customers look to you as the industry expert in areas related to your product or service. You bring instant credibility based on your title and scope. They assume you have visibility to a big sample set of experiences from your company's other customers. Customers want to hear from you so they can learn and bring that value back to their own businesses. Speaking confidently and persuasively on stage also creates an opportunity for your company's executive team to observe how you connect with your customers. Your speaking demonstrates that you know your customers and have intimate knowledge of the experiences they receive.

CAREER ACCELERATOR

Speaking at customer events helps you establish credibility, demonstrates your expertise, and builds your professional brand.

Create Content for Your Marketing Teams

Marketers are always looking for ways to create interesting stories that resonate with prospects and existing customers. You are very likely in a prime position to capture and share those nuggets of wisdom. Marketers would of course love customer stories that demonstrate use cases that deliver tremendous measurable value. Maybe you have these stories. If so, share them. But if not, you can still provide thought leadership in other ways. Maybe you can write a blog about your experience working with a group of customers to solve a problem. Perhaps you can record a webinar sharing a few customer stories about how they recognized value from your product or service.

Present at Industry Conferences or Business Meetups

A valuable way for you to become recognized as a thought leader beyond your company is to create opportunities to share your knowledge with industry peers. This does not necessarily mean that you need to invest time extensively building your brand or generating thousands of followers. It just means that you are putting yourself in situations where you can learn from others and where they can learn from you.

Keep an eye out for relevant conferences, functional meetups, or industry gatherings. Leading software companies commonly host conferences that can feel like industry get-togethers. Research firms also regularly host events or conferences that pull together industry experts. They often put out "calls for speakers" well ahead of the session. Submit your proposal and give it a shot!

Post on LinkedIn About Your Success Stories or Your Observations

One of the most effective ways to share information these days in a professional environment happens on LinkedIn. You are always only minutes away from sharing an insightful observation with your audience. What's stopping you? Don't get intimidated by seeing posts that generate dozens or hundreds of likes. You probably have important wisdom to share. Your customers could get inspired by seeing you personally sharing your insights on LinkedIn. They are learning from you and hearing examples of what works and doesn't work related to your product or service. Or maybe you have knowledge that helps them do their jobs better. You may also have employees that want to see you being present on LinkedIn as an indication that you are "leading from the front."

Participate in Webinars or Podcasts

With the recent transition of so many companies to a remote work environment, the cottage industry of hosting webinars and podcasts has never been more popular. The barrier to entry is almost non-existent. Everyone has a video camera and microphone in their workspaces. Even if you are not hosting the webinar or podcast yourself, there is a very good chance that your industry or function already has a set of ongoing channels.

For example, just the Customer Success function alone has dozens of different opportunities that you can find with a simple Google search. Reach out to the hosts and propose a topic. They are always looking for new speakers. You can also look into sessions hosted by companies that sell solutions to your industry. If you get anxious about public speaking on a stage or in front of a room of people, this can be a low-risk way to practice. For a list of podcasts for post-sale leaders, please visit www.ccoplaybook.com/resources.

What's in It for You?

Each of these opportunities to demonstrate your thought leadership builds value for your professional development. First, each opportunity presents a growing number of ways for you to share your knowledge with others who are interested in learning from you. Second, you will start to be recognized as an expert in one or more areas related to your field. People that may notice include your key customers, your peer leaders, your executive team, and future hiring managers. Third, sharing your knowledge will expose you to a wider network of thought leaders, industry experts, and functional peers with whom you can interact, learn, and share best practices. They may be people that can help you identify your next career opportunity, improve a business process, or refer potential candidates to you for an open position on your team.

CHAPTER REVIEW

QUESTIONS TO CONSIDER

- What are the areas where you have unique knowledge or understanding of your customers, business, function, or industry trends?
- What actions do you currently take to share your knowledge and experience with different groups of stakeholders such as customers, employees, and colleagues?
- What challenges or fears, if any, are currently holding you back from sharing your knowledge and expertise more broadly?
- What types of thought leadership opportunities have you considered in the past? Which have you pursued? Which have you deferred? Why?

ACTION PLAN

- Identify one to two areas of expertise that you could potentially share with your customers, employees, or colleagues in the next two to three months that would help them learn something important.
- Consider the format for how you could best share this knowledge with your intended audience. Review your proposal with the appropriate internal stakeholders or leaders.
- Define a timeline for delivering against this thought leadership opportunity. Hold yourself accountable for meeting this timeline.
- Provide the thought leadership to your intended audience in the agreed-upon format. Seek feedback from your audience to see if it had the intended impact.

Part 3

Action Plan and Trends to Consider

Accelerate Your Path to the Executive Table

In this book, you have now learned about the scope of the Chief Customer Officer role. You have read about the expectations placed on CCOs by their companies' executive teams. You have reviewed the eight skills and behaviors that effective CCOs need to master and maybe you have even completed the CCO Maturity Model™ assessment to identify strengths and gaps in your own experiences.

Putting Your Plan into Action

There are five challenges that I commonly see that hold people back. You can use these as a checklist to create an action plan to accelerate progress toward your career goals:

1. Your CEO and other executives don't understand the value of the CCO role.

2. You don't know what to do or what skills to work on to advance your career.

3. You don't speak up and advocate for yourself with your manager and executive team.

4. You are not looking at your role from the perspective of what the company expects.

5. You are not delivering the results and ROI your organization needs from you.

CAREER ACCELERATOR

Start working on your action plan today. Acknowledge your opportunities for growth and learning.

Challenge 1

Evolving leaders often need to take ownership of their own career development. Since the role of Chief Customer Officer is relatively new, there is not always a clear understanding of the expectations and outcomes for someone in this position. In addition, CEOs and CFOs may not have thought through how to measure the performance of a CCO or an aspiring CCO. They likely have experience measuring results for a sales, marketing, or product executive. But measuring the results of a CCO can often be unclear.

Maranda Dziekonski is a great example of someone who took responsibility to set expectations and define success metrics with her CEO. This directly led to her ultimate promotion to CCO.

"What I have done throughout my career is make it very clear to my manager, usually the CEO, what my goal is," she explained. "For example, I want to be an SVP, or I want to be a CCO. I then share what I think that means and what outcomes I want to deliver. We then can discuss whether those expectations and outcomes align with what they think I should be delivering."

Dziekonski joined Swiftly as the VP of Customer Success and People Operations. She had this type of discussion with her CEO and mapped out a plan along with a timeline to be considered for a CCO title.

She said, "Our plan revolved around achieving three major things – delivering strong NPS, gross retention rates, and net retention rates." By getting alignment with her CEO, she could now work toward these objectives with a shared understanding that if those expectations were met, that she would be a strong candidate for promotion.

Over the course of two years, Dziekonski was promoted first to a Senior Vice President title and then to a Chief Customer Officer position.

"Consistently, my team and I killed our numbers. It was a very measurable way to see that I was partnering and driving the right outcomes through my team," she said. She also made sure that the results her team was achieving were measurable and transparent to the company. If you want to be on a path to being promoted, you could do well to follow Dziekonski approach.

You too can be proactive to talk with your manager about what they expect from you and the criteria they will use to evaluate your performance. You can use the techniques you learned in this book as context for that discussion.

CHALLENGE #1
Your CEO and executives don't understand the value of the CCO role.

ACTION PLAN #1
Define expectations of the CCO role with them.

Challenge 2

The CCO Maturity Model™ is designed to help you assess your relative strengths and opportunities among the eight skills and behaviors that are most important for a Chief Customer Officer or aspiring CCO. The framework can help you identify where you are relative to the common expectations for leaders at different levels of an organization. You can then use the results to prioritize where you invest time for professional development and experiential learning. More about the CCO Maturity Model™ can be found at www.ccoplaybook.com/resources

CHALLENGE #2
You don't know what to do or what skills to work on to advance your career.

ACTION PLAN #2
Take the CCO Maturity Model assessment and develop an action plan based on the results.

Challenge 3

Catherine had been the Director of Customer Success at a leading healthcare services provider. She managed all of the post-sale organizations for her business and had a track record of consistently delivering strong results against her target metrics. But she was frustrated and disappointed because her peers were getting promoted to Vice President, and she wasn't.

Wasn't her work to quietly improve Net Retention Rate enough? Apparently not. She said that her manager wanted her to be more effective at highlighting the work of her team to show its impact on the company-level results. "They want me to be more in the spotlight. They really find value in the flashy stuff," she explained.

One of her direct reports provided additional context: "She is a great leader. She is extremely strategic and intelligent. She does great things and probably should get recognized for them. But she isn't one to make herself stand out." Her company leaders expected Catherine to be able to more effectively communicate the value of her organization as a driver of company results.

So Catherine identified a number of initiatives that she could lead to raise the visibility of her organization on company-level initiatives – creating a Customer Advisory Board, providing prioritized feedback to the product team on improvement opportunities, sharing customer stories at company all-hands meetings, and creating case studies of how customer ARR grows due to the work of her organization. She intends to then make sure that she effectively communicates the results of these initiatives to the right audiences and in public settings.

For leaders like Catherine, sharing results like these isn't about tooting your own horn. Sharing these accomplishments is about making sure that you are simply connecting the dots for your company's executive team to show the value of what you and your team do on a daily basis. Importantly, you need to connect your efforts to how your company generates revenue or improves profitability.

So much of the work of a post-sale leader is behind the scenes, ensuring that processes are functioning as expected and preventing bad things from happening. Resolve support tickets. Prevent customers from churning. Get customers implemented quickly and efficiently. This work isn't always flashy or exciting. Yes, you often end up in the spotlight. But just as often, you are in the spotlight because something goes wrong.

You need to find ways to effectively communicate the positive results and progress of your organization. It doesn't mean that you hide the bad stuff. You just need to find opportunities to highlight the good stuff as well, particularly when there are important benefits to your company when you share those results and stories.

CHALLENGE #3
You don't speak up and advocate for yourself with your CEO, executive team and peers.

ACTION PLAN #3
Create opportunities to share your results publicly, take credit for outcomes and make your voice heard.

Challenge 4

Eduarda Camacho has been the Chief Customer Officer for BMC Software for a year. Prior to joining BMC, she had been the Chief Customer Officer at PTC, another global software and services provider. Eduarda had thoughtfully worked her way up through the PTC organization for over 20 years before taking on the CCO role.

It wasn't a particularly direct path to the C-suite. Over her long career at PTC, Eduarda had worked in a number of different business units and led a variety of functional departments. She paid close attention to how the various departments interacted with each other and studied how they worked together to deliver results.

"One of the things that benefited me was that I worked in so many different organizations at PTC that I was able to connect the dots pretty well," she said. "If you want to be a CCO, you have to be able to understand the whole company and all the different functions. You need to be able to connect the dots."

When she joined BMC as Chief Customer Officer, she quickly demonstrated her value as a high-impact leader by thinking about how her organization could contribute to company-level results.

She said, "When I came to BMC, I tried to really make sure that I understood what's really happening behind each of those functions so you can bring the customer to them. You can speak their language of why they may need to do something different for the customer. You cannot just be a functional leader in your space. You have to bring more to the table."

CCOs and aspiring CCOs need to recognize how the work of their organizations contributes to the achievement of company goals. The more you can internalize how the various levers across the company interact to provide value to customers and shareholders, the more likely it is that you can succeed in your executive-level role.

CHALLENGE #4

You look at your organization's outcomes independently from their impact on company results.

ACTION PLAN #4

You understand how your organization interacts with other functions to deliver results that impact company performance.

Challenge 5

I'm still surprised how often customer-facing leaders miss opportunities to improve their business results because they don't take advantage of the best-practice expertise that exists. At a certain leadership level, perhaps executives feel like they are expected to have all the answers themselves. They may have dozens or even (in some cases) hundreds of employees on their teams. Of course, if you just put those heads together, you will come up with the best practices, right? Unfortunately, that isn't how the situation commonly plays out.

Chief Marketing Officers think nothing of spending tens or hundreds of thousands of dollars on outside consulting expertise and agencies to help them create content, run events, and execute marketing campaigns. There is a plethora of peer communities for CMOs and marketing leaders.

Sales executives similarly hire sales trainers, leverage motivational speakers, and collaborate through networks of other sales leaders to get best practices into place.

But from what I observed with hundreds of CCOs and aspiring CCOs I have interacted with, these leaders are generally reluctant to ask for help or to set aside consulting budgets for outside experts. Perhaps they believe that their CEOs expect them to be an expert in each of the functional areas within their span of control. Maybe they are embarrassed to admit that they don't know the KPIs and how to pull the levers necessary to improve the business results.

Strong executives know when to supplement their own expertise. That is why you hire talented leaders to report to you. That is why you should reach out to your peers that have experience when faced with similar challenges. That is why you should hire expert consultants to supplement and supercharge the work of your team.

CHALLENGE #5

You aren't sure how to achieve business results that are expected by your CEO or CFO, so you wing it.

ACTION PLAN #5

Get help from your peer network or expert consultants that have tackled this challenge before.

CHAPTER REVIEW

QUESTIONS TO CONSIDER

- What challenges do you face as you work to achieve your professional development goals?
- Have you discussed these challenges with your manager or CEO? Why or why not? What was the outcome of that discussion?
- What are the criteria that your manager will use to determine if you are ready to be promoted? Have you discussed the criteria and potential timeline with your manager?
- What action steps, improvements, or results are you expected to achieve for you to be considered for a promotion?

ACTION PLAN

- Discuss your career goals with your manager in the next 30 to 60 days.
- Work with your manager to define the promotion criteria that would get you to the next level.
- Identify opportunities to grow your capabilities and close any gaps in the skills required for you to operate at the next level of your organization.
- Ask for resources that could assist you to deliver the expected business results and to develop the executive-level skills required to get promoted into a future role. This could include external consulting, internal hiring, or other leadership development opportunities.

Predictions and Industry Trends

So where are things headed for the Chief Customer Officer role? Like many other executive positions, staying current will require you to pay attention to industry trends and best practices. Here are a few trends that I anticipate you should keep an eye on in the next three to five years.

1. CCOs Will Have Increased Accountability for Revenue and Profitability Targets

I expect that the role of the Chief Customer Officer will become increasingly focused on the commercial and financial outcomes they deliver across their teams. While metrics like NPS, adoption health, and CSAT will still be important, CCOs will need to be able to demonstrate the impact of their teams on revenue growth, operating margins, and company profitability.

CCOs will increasingly have direct accountability for teams responsible for customer renewals and revenue expansion. Their teams will need to aggressively invest in training, automation, and self-service resources that allow them to support a larger number of customers without adding headcount at the same rate. This also means that CCOs should expect higher overall compensation packages commensurate with this financial accountability. However, they should also expect that a higher percentage of their compensation will be variable and based on how they perform against their financial targets.

2. AI and Machine Learning Will Help Teams Be More Predictive and Prescriptive

Over the next several years, I expect that artificial intelligence and machine learning solutions will become more prevalent in post-sale functions. They will offer customer-facing teams the ability to provide more relevant recommendations and next steps based on the behavior and trends of similar customers. For example, these solutions can help success management teams be more predictive in identifying at-risk clients and recommending next steps to address the issue. Renewals and expansion selling teams can use these capabilities to more easily identify the "next-best product or service" to help your company grow NRR. Support teams will use these solutions to anticipate potential problems before they even happen and suggest ways to prevent them. Customer Education teams can recommend the right training video or learning path for new and existing customers. AI and machine learning have the potential to be key contributors to CCOs' ability to scale their organizations in a cost-efficient way.

3. Technology Solutions Will Consolidate and Talk to Each Other

The technology stack available for organizations under the CCO's responsibility is pretty broad. I have published tech stack recommendations you can review at www.ccoplaybook.com/resources.

There are an incredibly wide number of solution categories available ranging from a support case management system to a customer success platform to a customer onboarding solution to an education service learning management system. Those are just a few of the big-ticket items. Then you have the time tracking systems, the resource management platforms, the data analytics tools, project management tools, and internal communication platforms. The list goes on and on.

Each of these solutions has different functional buyers within the post-sale organizations. But ultimately, they will need to be approved, budgeted for, and often implemented and supported by the CCO and their team. I expect that these software vendors will find ways to make the buying, implementation, and management process better through industry consolidation and integrations across tech stack categories. By having a common decision-maker in the CCO, these software vendors will also be able to sell a broader range of product solutions to their customers.

4. The Customer Operations Leader Role Will Be a Steppingstone to a CCO Role

In an earlier chapter, I outlined the responsibilities of the Customer Operations organization. It is a team that is commonly responsible for creating reports and dashboards, implementing and maintaining the software solutions used across a CCO's organization, managing the operations reviews, driving cross-functional improvement projects, and optimizing resource management within each department.

The leader of this Customer Operations team is often the right-hand person collaborating with the Chief Customer Officer to understand financial results, business trends, and opportunities for improvement. I believe that the skills and experiences that a Customer Operations leader will develop are extremely valuable for becoming a Chief Customer Officer. Aspiring CCOs would do well to consider doing a stint leading a Customer Operations team.

5. CCOs Will Take Accountability for Customer Marketing

I believe that a growing number of companies will move the Customer Marketing function from under the Chief Marketing Officer into the CCO's organization. Many marketing organizations are primarily structured around driving new sales for the company. This leaves a customer marketing organization as an afterthought. For post-sale teams to get the attention of customer marketers, they often have to beg and borrow to get even a sliver of the marketers' time.

However, the skills of these customer marketers are critical for the successful delivery of customer-facing experiences at scale. The marketers are potentially experts at using automation to communicate with customers at the right time and with the right message based on what your company knows about them. They understand how to tell impactful stories that can be used to help drive customer behavior to adopt your new products or services, understand the value they are receiving, or how to benefit from additional use cases. They are data-driven and effectively use metrics to inform their decisions. I also believe that managing the customer community could fall under their scope. All of these characteristics could be extremely beneficial to the various functions within a CCO's scope of responsibility.

6. CCOs Will Recognize the Value of Hiring Outside Specialists and Experts

I believe that CCOs and their functional leaders are missing out on tremendous opportunities to accelerate growth and profitability in their organizations because they are not hiring outside experts to help them with their strategy and operational execution. In contrast, Chief Marketing Officers think nothing of spending millions of dollars on outside digital agencies, branding experts, content development writers, or event organizers. They build fees for consultants and marketing agencies into their budgets and benefit from getting the expertise they need at exactly the time they need it. On the other hand, I have observed that CCOs and their leadership teams generally resist looking outside their organizations for specialized assistance.

One hypothesis is that the post-sale functions have become so dependent on the people in their organization to scale that when the budgeting process comes along, the leaders feel like they have to focus on using a budget to add the bodies they think they will need to support the business goals. They are less confident about the improved productivity or efficiency they will get from working with outside experts to define a new strategy, train their teams, supplement their workforce, or project manage certain one-time initiatives.

I believe that CCOs will soon recognize that they can more effectively contribute to higher revenue and profitability by leveraging specialized expertise to get the help they need just when they need it, rather than by only thinking about adding full-time headcount. They will start to build those placeholders into their annual budget.

7. More CCOs Will Report Directly to CEOs

As a broader cohort of customer-facing leaders develop executive-level skills and deliver company-impacting results, CEOs will become more comfortable adding them to their executive staff. The leader of your customer-facing organizations should absolutely have a seat at the executive table. However, many companies currently have post-sale leaders that are not yet operating at the level expected from an individual that reports to the CEO. This is one of the reasons I wrote this book.

That isn't a dig on the CCO profession. It is just a reality that this post-sale leadership role is relatively new for many companies. This means that many post-sale executives are stepping into bigger and bigger roles pretty quickly.

The impact of this trend is that many post-sale executives with a VP, SVP, and even sometimes a CCO title are now reporting directly to Chief Revenue Officers, Sales leaders, or Chief Operating Officers. You can learn a lot from reporting to one of these executives. They are potentially excellent managers, operational leaders, and experienced change management drivers. Plus, they likely have more time to provide executive-level coaching, feedback, and mentorship.

However, as post-sale leaders mature in their profession, I expect that a higher percentage of CCOs will be invited to report directly to the CEOs of their companies. The CCOs' performance and impact will be comparable to that of their peers, and they will have earned that seat at the executive table. Will you be someone who reports to the CEO?

8. A Growing Number of CCOs Will Become CEOs

I am convinced that the skills necessary to be a great Chief Customer Officer are also the type of skills that could make you a strong candidate to be a CEO. You understand the financials. You recognize customer needs. You work well cross-functionally. You think strategically. You create change. You drive revenue growth and improve profitability. You communicate effectively with various stakeholders including at the board level. Tack on a few other experiences along the way in your career, and the CEO role can be in your sights.

I am particularly interested to see which CCOs out there take on this CEO position over the next few years. I hope it will be you.

Your Next Steps

First, I want to thank you for reading this book. I am honored to be part of your career journey. Just picking up this book and reading it to the end tells me that you are serious about developing your career as a customer-facing executive. You now have the roadmap you need to succeed.

Second, realizing that this is just the beginning is important. Whether you have been a Chief Customer Officer for years or are just starting to take on leadership roles on a potential career path to CCO someday, you can start implementing the strategies in this book right now.

In fact, I'd encourage you to go to www.ccoplaybook.com/resources right now to access all of the additional templates, worksheets, and best practice resources I've talked about throughout this book. Doing so will give you everything you need to succeed beyond these pages.

Last, if you don't want to do this alone, or if you feel that you or someone on your leadership team could benefit from some personal attention, please reach out to me at rod@hellocco.com to learn more about my advisory and consulting services. Working together one-on-one can help you and your team accelerate your career progression and expand your business impact.

In addition, since delivering consistently strong results is essential to growing your career, know that I can also partner with you and your team on consulting projects to help you make faster progress on your most important post-sale strategic initiatives.

Great leaders know when to leverage outside expertise to accelerate results delivery and prevent predictable mistakes. If you're looking for help in these areas, I would love to help you.

Whether you do this all on your own or seek out my help, I want you to know that YOU can do this – I know you can! Please let me know how you progress and how this book has helped you on this journey.

See you in the executive suite!

Rod

About the Author

Rod Cherkas is the CEO and Founder of HelloCCO, a strategy consulting firm based in San Mateo, California that serves clients worldwide. He is the leading global advisor to Chief Customer Officers and their post-sale leaders. His vast experience helps CEOs, CCOs, and their executive teams increase customer retention rates, accelerate time to value, expand revenue faster, and improve financial performance.

Rod has been a customer-facing executive at several of Silicon Valley's most customer-centric companies including Intuit, RingCentral, Marketo, and Gainsight, helping these last three to achieve more than $1 billion IPOs or exits. He is also an Operating Advisor to CCOs and post-sale executives at the Warburg Pincus portfolio of companies.

A Philadelphia native, Rod completed his bachelor's degree in Economics at Duke University and received his MBA at the Stanford Graduate School of Business. Rod and his wife, Corey, live in San Mateo, California and have three children.

You can stay connected with Rod on social media or through email:

- Follow him on LinkedIn: www.linkedin.com/in/rodcherkas/.
- Send him an email: rod@hellocco.com.
- Keep up with his latest thought leadership by signing up for his newsletter at www.rodcherkas.com.
- Learn more about his consulting and advisory services at www.rodcherkas.com.

Looking for a Speaker or Facilitator for Your Next Customer Event or Strategy Offsite?

Could you benefit from having an experienced, customer-facing professional help you design and host a quarterly planning offsite, facilitate a leadership team working session, moderate a strategic workshop, or execute a customer advisory board event?

Rod Cherkas is an experienced, passionate, and relatable speaker and facilitator that offers the following services:

- Consulting and Workshop Facilitation
- "Walk in your Customer's Shoes" experiences
- Post-Sale Strategic Planning Offsite Facilitation
- Moderate a Customer Panel
- Keynote Presentations
- Customer Advisory Board meetings

To hire Rod for your next event or to discuss potential experiences that add value for your customer-facing leadership team, email rod@hellocco.com.

Acknowledgments

To Corey, my wife, for encouragement, support, and kindness over my career as I accumulated these experiences, bounced back from setbacks, and took on new challenges. Most of all, thank you for being a role model and mother to our kids. I couldn't have written this book without you.

Thank you to my children Zack, Shelby, and Marlee. You demonstrate that with your own hard work and creativity, you can accomplish anything. That inspired me as I wrote a book for the first time.

To my brothers, Michael and Kevin, and to my Uncle Gary for helping me and my family navigate life's challenges. And for always making us feel so loved and welcome even when we lived far away.

Thank you to:

Nick Mehta and Dan Steinman, who helped create a profession and career path for those of us who love to design great customer experiences, deliver company-impacting results, and drive innovation.

Jason Holmes for being an amazing mentor as a CCO, people manager, and career coach. You brought me into two positions that were transformative for me professionally and personally.

Sue Heilbronner for helping me define my career roadmap and for inspiring me to start my own consulting business. Coming up with the "HelloCCO" name and branding was just brilliant!

Lisa Larter for the business expertise you have shared that developed me into a better consultant, speaker, and thought leader. You understand me and push me to be uncomfortable.

Robbie Baxter for your advice to find my niche as an independent consultant and for showing me a path to write a book that advances a profession.

Dan Janal for your guidance on how to write a book, your ongoing encouragement, and your masterful editing of this book. You made me a better writer every time we spoke.

Weston Lyon and Tracey Miller for the brilliant design, proofreading, and publishing of this book. Your advice and expertise have been spot-on as you turned these words into a beautiful resource.

Sharon Holmes for your ability to translate my ideas and words into appealing visuals that enable my audiences to quickly grasp the concepts and frameworks.

The many people who reviewed my manuscript and provided insightful assistance, suggestions, and feedback: Chris Hicken, Mary Poppen, Laura Lakhwara, Gözde Görce, Gemma Cipriani-Espineira, Anita Toth, Rachel Rozen, Star Hofer, Brian Hartley, Omid Razavi, Karla Kannan, Austin Gardner, Christine Rimer, Rebecca Heyman, Mathilde Sanson, Michael Horsley, Michael Lee, Marko Müller, Hannah Thompson, Ben Collier, Jennifer Baca, Laurence Leong, Tiffany Taylor, Paula Sobb, Angie Grech Holt, Amit Kandpal, Robert Padron, Srikrishnan Ganesan, Mike Gospe, Inger Rarick, Karen Bros, Irene Lefton, Ashna Patel, and Ryan Dalton. Each of you contributed to making this book better for our peers.

The incredible thought leaders, executives, and investors who shared their wealth of expertise and stories with me and whose insight elevates this book: Chris Hicken, David Sakamoto, Shari Srebnick, Kristi Faltorusso, Layton Chaney, Maranda Dziekonski, Nick Mehta, Christine Rimer, Gemma Cipriani-Espineira, Sean Jacobsohn, Kellie Capote, Anita Toth, Alex Rexroad, Matt Dempsey, Star Hofer, Mary Poppen, Dan Steinman, Rob Schmeltzer, Tiffany Taylor, Jenn Chester, Roxy Hoffman, Todd Watts, Justin Sadrian, Jordan Mace, Fergal Campbell, Deniz Omurgonulsen Altuğ, Chad Quinn, David Reiling, Michelle Hackett, Eduarda Camacho, Sridhar Gollapalli, Rachel Orston, Wyeth Goodenough, Chitra Madhwacharyula, Ellie Wu, Samma Hafeez, and Shannah Van Winkle.

The hundreds of Chief Customer Officers and aspiring Chief Customer Officers I have met who work tirelessly for your customers, your employees, your colleagues, and your shareholders. I see you. I hear you. I appreciate all that you do every day. I love how you drive constant innovation, learn quickly, and share your best practices with others.

A few of the outstanding managers who took a chance on me and brought me into their company as an employee over the years. I was so lucky to have met you and made a connection in a way that made you confident enough to hire me. I learned so much from you and appreciate that you took a risk on me: Ellen Perelman, David Sipes, Jason Holmes, and Ashvin Vaidyanathan.

To Scott Cook, Intuit's Co-Founder, with whom I had the opportunity to work with, observe, and learn from for almost fifteen years. You role modeled the importance of designing for customer delight, walking in your customers' shoes, building highly engaged teams, and driving rapid experimentation.

Index

Made in the USA
Monee, IL
23 January 2023

25981798R00144